HIDDEN
HISTORY
of
OLD ATLANTA

HIDDEN
HISTORY
of
OLD ATLANTA

Mark Pifer

Foreword *by* Jim Auchmutey

THE
History
PRESS

Published by The History Press
Charleston, SC
www.historypress.com

Front cover: A view looking South down Whitehall Street (also known as the Sandtown Trail) in 1864. *Library of Congress*.

First published 2021

Manufactured in the United States

ISBN 9781467146074

Library of Congress Control Number: 2020945743

Notice: The information in this book is true and complete to the best of our knowledge. It is offered without guarantee on the part of the author or The History Press. The author and The History Press disclaim all liability in connection with the use of this book.

To the people who built the Georgia railroads with their hands and did more than anyone else to create a great new city in the South but received very little of the reward or the recognition for having done it.

To my wife, Robin, and my girls, Ava and Sasha, who inspire me every day to follow a dream.

Contents

CONTENTS

FOREWORD

In three decades as a reporter and editor at the *Atlanta Journal-Constitution*, I occasionally heard new hires from out of town say that Atlanta didn't have much history. As a native of the city, born at Saint Joseph's Infirmary when it was downtown, I would take offense. "No history?" I'd say. "Only if you think the Civil War and the civil rights movement aren't historic."

But I knew what they meant. Atlanta is young as major American cities go, and it has always looked to the future, regrettably tearing down a good many of its fine old buildings in the name of progress. Compared to Boston or New Orleans, I suppose this would seem to some newcomers like a suburbosphere with no past.

Well, we most certainly have a past, and I didn't know the half of it.

In this book, Mark Pifer focuses on prehistoric Atlanta—a term that had never crossed my mind—to document the evolution of the area before the Civil War, the place where popular imaginings of our saga usually begin.

He starts millions of years ago with geology and tectonic shifts, when Georgia literally faced West Africa, and moves on to zoology and the era when dinosaurs roamed the Southeast. Who knew there was a local creature called the Appalachiosaur, a T-rex cousin who was more fearsome because it had arms long enough to grab its prey?

The Asian immigrants we first called Indians and then Native Americans arrived ages later, moving into the area that became Atlanta some four thousand years ago. We live with their place names every day—Cherokee County, the Chattahoochee River—but few of us know much more about them than the vague memory that they were forced to leave Georgia to make way for interlopers. I certainly didn't know that in 1825, Creek factions fought a bloody battle in what soon became central Atlanta.

The city we inhabit is rooted, of course, in railroads, which came to this part of Georgia during the 1840s and soon brought commerce and thousands of settlers. Early Atlanta could be as seedy as a seaport, only instead of ships and sailors it had trains and railroad men. It teemed with gambling, thievery, cockfighting and prostitution. At one point, there was one prostitute for every dozen men. Much of the vice was concentrated in a section called Snake Nation, near today's Castleberry Hill, which was burned to the ground by a vigilante group representing a political bloc that called itself the Moral Party.

I was particularly interested, as a student of barbecue history, to learn that Atlanta's first homicide occurred after a political barbecue at Walton Spring, for which Spring Street is named. Two partisans who attended the festivities confronted each other later that day outside a tavern on Decatur Street, and one stabbed the other fatally with a six-inch knife. I've walked past the sites of the barbecue and the killing a hundred times and never knew their significance.

When you think about it, history is like Stone Mountain. We focus on the huge rock we can see and never think much about all the underground granite we cannot see. There's so much buried. Mark Pifer has unearthed a fascinating view of the hidden foundation Atlanta was built on.

—Jim Auchmutey, author of *Smokelore: A Short History of Barbecue in America* and *The Class of '65: A Student, a Divided Town, and the Long Road to Forgiveness*

ACKNOWLEDGEMENTS

As I put the final touches on this book and think about how to acknowledge the many people who helped make it reality, it is my fiftieth birthday. I hadn't planned for this to be the day I finished the book, but I suppose it is a very appropriate day to think about acknowledgements. Perhaps, as Freud said, there are no accidents, and I saved this part of the book for my birthday without realizing it. The usual traditions for a fiftieth birthday as I understand them are that it should be a day of reflection on my years or that I should cast about in a sudden existential crisis. Who am I? What am I doing? Will anything I have done ever matter?

I'm happy to say any of those panicky thoughts I might have had were quashed some time ago. I can then give you my not-so-sagacious advice on my day 19,263 on this planet. The best advice I have if you should ever question your place in the universe at any point of your life is to start reading or writing a book about history. While you might think concentration on our planet's and our country's long history might make you feel smaller and less significant, history teaches the opposite when properly understood. It is the ideal way to realize you play an important part in a story that you may not have even realized was unfolding around you.

I was not born in the South, but I have now spent most of my life here. I will always love where I grew up, but I'm proud to be the southerner I chose to be, and I love Atlanta. It has given my family and me a wonderful, happy life. This book and the greater understanding of those who came before me and our similarities to one another has made me feel more a natural part of the city's next chapter.

The story of Atlanta and how it came to be is longer than most people realize. More people of all kinds have had an important role in that story than anyone would guess. Many of them didn't do so by choice, and many of them never heard of a place called Atlanta. They were central characters in the story nevertheless, and it is those people's lives that interest us most and with which we most identify: the desperate, the determined and the discontent. The story continues. We are all part of many stories bigger than what we can see around us from day to day. People will see that and remember us too.

With that, it seems appropriate to first thank my parents for creating me fifty years ago and for everything they and the rest of my family have done since then to nurture the interest in history and writing that led to this book. Our family cherishes its unique history. I was raised to be curious about it and to take as much delight (often more delight) in the unflattering parts as the flattering parts of our history. Here we are, still learning who we are.

I could thank my wife for so many, many things she has done. Today, as I complete this book, I thank her for being my inspiration, my chief supporter, my lead editor and my creative consultant, without whom I'd still be trying to decide what to write about.

I thank my children, Ava and Sasha, for supporting me in my struggles and triumphs, as I try to support them in theirs. I will never stop doing things I think will make them proud.

Jim Auchmutey has become my mentor in the world of professional writing. His encouragement that I can do this and his advice about how to become a better writer have been invaluable. I also, of course, thank him for the wonderful foreword he wrote and all of his support of my budding career as a writer.

I thank the network of local historians who have come before me and left behind the pieces of the story that I simply knitted together and festooned as best I could, especially Vivian Price, Franklin Garrett, George Gilman Smith, Wilbur Kurtz and Carl T. Hudgins. I also thank everyone at the Atlanta History Center and the DeKalb History Center for their kind assistance and resources.

I also thank Joe Gartrell of The History Press for his enthusiasm, advice and support in making this book a reality. "Louis, this is the beginning of a beautiful friendship."

Introduction

All roads lead to Rome. It's a wonderful expression. It says a lot in just five words. Normally, it's used as a figurative expression, not a literal one. All the roads that led to Rome were elements of society like politics, science, philosophy and commerce. In the case of Atlanta and the story of its creation, the same expression could be used much more literally. For a long time, all roads in the Southeast led to Atlanta. This was true even long before there was the wisp of an idea for a city that would become Atlanta. Humankind has used the area as a hub in every era of human history in North America. It was then chosen as the main hub in the state of Georgia for the railroads. Next came the major highways. Interstates 85, 75 and 20 all meet in Atlanta. Next came the airlines.

In discussions of Atlanta's origins, it is often pointed out that there were two cities in the South considered for the construction of a hub for Delta Airlines: Atlanta and Birmingham, Alabama. In 1970, the Birmingham metro area was about half the size of Atlanta. It had a population of about 700,000 compared to 1.4 million in the Atlanta area. The decision to locate the new hub in Atlanta occurred in 1986. Both cities have grown since then, but today, Atlanta has grown to be about five times the size of Birmingham and a crossroads directly connected to the entire world. Atlanta has a population of over 6 million. The Birmingham area has around 1.2 million residents. Crossroads connect. They connect people and new ideas. They also bring money that builds cities.

This map shows many of the features that existed in Georgia before the arrival of Europeans including the major trails and its ancient coastline. *Sketch by the author from several sources.*

The comparison of Atlanta and Birmingham is an interesting story but obviously oversimplifies the combination of factors that lead to the growth of a city. Unlike the neatly laid out trails running into Atlanta in 1830, the road the city itself has traveled to become the capital of Georgia—and arguably the capital of the South—has been very messy and meandering. It snaked its way through centuries of rugged landscape until it arrived at the settling of a new major city.

I

THE BRIEF HISTORY OF ATLANTA BEFORE PEOPLE

E arth moves. Its landmasses are constantly surging up and down. The continents are drifting and spinning around the globe, and occasionally they meet. When they do, there is a slow-motion cataclysm as two continents are welded into one. New bedrock forms hundreds of miles inland from where they met. Volcanoes rise and spew rocks hundreds of miles.

The last time this happened in Georgia was around three hundred million years ago. Every piece of land on Earth was slowly joined into one great, massive piece of land: Pangaea. When the land that would become Atlanta began pushing up onto the landscape, lava jetted out and was thrown as far inland as the Mississippi River. The Appalachian Mountains were thrown up. Atlanta's land slowly emerged out of the water and then rose high up in these mountains.

When the continents finally began to separate two hundred million years ago, a large piece of the continent of Africa broke off and was left attached to North America. Florida and large parts of southern Georgia, southern Alabama and the Bahamas are actually pieces left behind when Africa pulled away from North America.

Over the past two hundred million years, the land has been worn down by time, wind and water. The high, craggy Appalachians have been worn and smoothed. The continents have continued to spin and slide across the planet. The hills and mountains have continued to churn up and down. In several places in the area that would become Atlanta, new

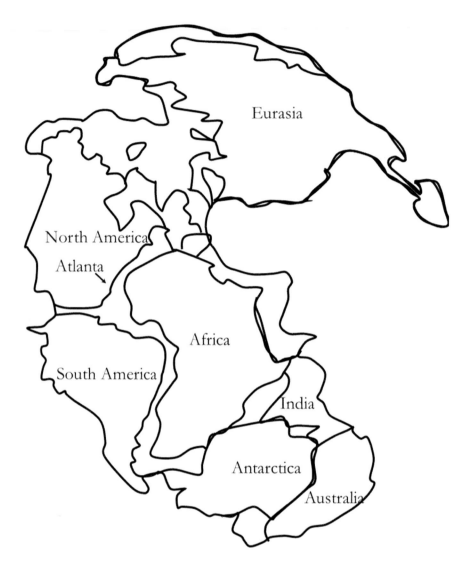

Some three hundred million years ago, Georgia was connected with Africa, specifically to what is now Liberia and Sierra Leone. *Sketch by the author using Wikimedia Commons.*

intrusions of rock pushed their way into the bedrock, creating granite. As the land around the granite was worn away, these pockets remained on the landscape in places like Stone Mountain, Panola Mountain, Arabia Mountain and Kennesaw Mountain. Water trickled out of the hills and dug into the landscape, forming major streams and rivers. Southeastern

North America became a long, undulating hillside gradually giving out to the Gulf of Mexico and the Atlantic Ocean.

While the landscape was slowly changing, the environment of Earth has changed many times as well. At times, it was much colder than it is now. Ice reached from the North Pole nearly as far south as where Atlanta is now. Other times, it has been much warmer, and the planet's ice melted to the point the oceans rose as much as 850 feet deeper than today. The beach was sometimes located where Macon is now.

Unlike most of the rest of the planet, the land near what is now Atlanta has stayed above water when the oceans rose and remained free of ice when the planet cooled. This is part of what made it an exceptionally pleasant place for life. Dinosaurs flourished in the rolling landscape during the late Cretaceous period between 145 and 66 million years ago. The rolling hills hosted droves of Lophorhothons, a type of duckbilled herbivore, and fleet-footed ornithomimids, an ostrich-like long-necked dinosaur. The king carnivore hunting them was the Appalachiosaur, a very close cousin to the Tyrannosaurus rex. Unlike the T-rex, the South's Appalachiosaur had long arms for grasping its prey like an attacking lion. If you want to get a good sense of what this monster really looked like you can visit a nearly complete skeleton of the Appalachiosaur in the McWane Museum in Alabama.

An Appalachiosaur takes down one of prehistoric Atlanta's Lophorhothons. *Illustrations by Chulsan Um.*

The Cretaceous dinosaurs disappeared sixty-six million years ago when massive asteroids slammed into the planet, altering its climate for millions of years. Nearly every animal on the planet bigger than a dog starved. Two of the only relatively large survivors of this cataclysm are still residing in Georgia today. These are the alligators and leatherback sea turtles.

The next peak in the diversity of life in the ancient Atlanta area occurred during the Pleistocene period between 2.5 million and 12,000 years ago. It was nestled into the high, rolling foothills of the Appalachians. Clear, cold streams and rivers rolled out of the mountains like they do farther north today. Evergreens and hardwoods, interspersed with grassy meadows, covered the landscape. It was an ideal haven for animals between ice to the north and ocean to the south.

Around 2.8 million years ago, North America became accessible from South America when additional tectonic events created the Isthmus of Panama. Later, colder temperatures lowered the oceans and exposed a new landmass between North America and Asia. Animals then began to migrate out of Europe and Asia into North America. The animals that arrived from the south through the Isthmus of Panama and from the north across Beringia all met in the Southeast with the animals that had evolved in North America, like the American mastodons, Yukon horses and Yukon camels. Many people are surprised to learn that the first horses and the first camels to appear on Earth emerged in the cold, northern climates of North America 30 to 50 million years ago. The traits that make a camel well suited as a desert beast of burden were adaptations that developed in the steppe-tundra of the Yukon where it originated. North America became one of the most diverse and astonishing ecosystems in the history of the world, and Atlanta's prehistoric landscape was located right in the middle of it.

The long-legged grazers were probably the first big animals to arrive in large numbers. There were bison, camels, caribou, moose, sheep, antelopes, muskox, short-legged horses, large-headed llamas and, of course, deer.

The abundant varieties of prey attracted an astonishing variety of predators. Every ice age super predator that fires our imagination today was present in the area. It didn't just host the smaller variety of saber-toothed cat. It also had the true, ferocious saber-toothed tigers prowling the banks of the Chattahoochee. The American lion that once hunted the forests of prehistoric Atlanta was very like a modern African lion but much larger. There were also cougars, lynx, margays (now found mainly in South America), ocelots, jaguars and fisher cats.

The giant chipmunk that lived during the Pleistocene era has only been found in Georgia. *Illustrations by Chulsan Um.*

There was a wider variety of bears than exists today, including black bears, brown bears and two extinct species called the Florida cave bear and the giant short-faced bear. The giant short-faced bear that once walked the woods of what would be Atlanta was the largest land predator to ever walk the Earth, about twice the size of the mighty polar bear, today's largest land predator.

Like it is today, prehistoric Atlanta was also a very dog-friendly place twenty thousand years ago. There were red wolves, red foxes, gray wolves, gray foxes, coyotes and dire wolves running wild. Among the true giants that arrived were mammoths, mastodon, giant bison, giant beavers, glyptodonts (giant armadillos), giant ground sloths and the ferocious giant chipmunk, a cat-sized chipmunk that has so far only been found to have lived in Georgia.

2

ATLANTA'S FIRST RESIDENTS

P eople first made their way into North America around fourteen thousand years ago. They then began to appear in the Southeast about twelve thousand years ago. Both plants and animals migrated over from Asia, and the people eventually followed them. Their favorite meals seem to have been the big mammals like mammoths, mastodons, bison, ground sloths, giant armadillos, tapirs, horses, wild pigs and caribou. Ancient bones of various Pleistocene animals have been found with the signs of having been killed and butchered by Pleistocene hunters.

The closest known and excavated Pleistocene sites of human activity to Atlanta are in Barnett Shoals near Athens, in the Ocmulgee National Monument near Macon and on Horse Leg Mountain near Rome. Pleistocene spear points have been found all over the Southeast, including around Lake Allatoona and Lake Lanier. Of course, neither lake existed during the Pleistocene. They were created when the Chattachoochee and Etowah Rivers were dammed in the 1940s and '50s. Spear points revealed on the shores of these lakes were uncovered by the rising and lowering water levels. Pleistocene artifacts could be found along any river or major creek bank in Georgia.

Once they settled in America, the culture of the Pleistocene hunter-gatherers began to change almost immediately. The world was rapidly warming up. The land was developing into the mild climate of the South today. Even more important, the larger game was rapidly disappearing. All of the giant animals like mastodons, saber-toothed tigers and glyptodonts

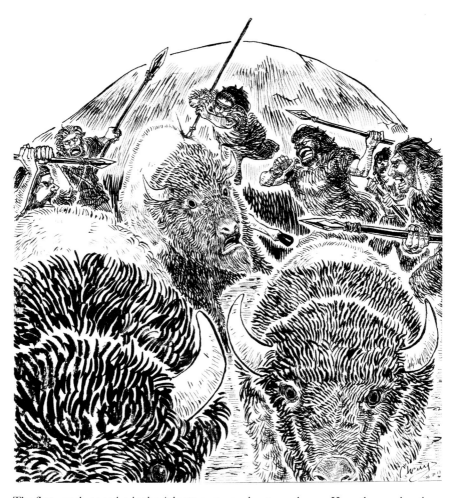

The first people to arrive in the Atlanta area were hunter-gatherers. Here, they are hunting bison under the shadow of Stone Mountain. *Illustrations by Chulsan Um.*

rapidly disappeared off the planet simultaneously across the globe. This was undoubtedly due, at least in large part, to the warming of the planet and the changing environment. The success of these early hunters could have also accelerated the demise of the Pleistocene's incredible megafauna.

As the people adjusted to the changing environment, they began to act in more similar ways to how we think of Indians in America. They stopped moving around as much as they had before and built semipermanent homes using wooden posts and thatch.

Their diet became much more varied. They hunted everything people hunt in Georgia today and some things they don't, including turkey, bear, opossum, raccoon, duck, muskrat, beaver, turtle and nearly anything else that moved. Deer hunting became a tent pole of their entire culture, a skill that would later be prized by the Europeans and then exploited to the point it became one of the core reasons for the collapse of Indian society.

About four thousand years ago, the people hunting and fishing in and around the northern Chattahoochee learned about the uses of soapstone. This led to another important cultural shift for the people in the area. Soapstone has several unique qualities that made it very useful, especially before the invention of pottery. First, it is very resistant to erosion because it is nonporous. Water can't get down inside of it, freeze and break it apart. Despite its resistance to water erosion and the acids and alkalis that normally break down stone, it is soft and very workable. It can be easily carved into shapes and hold water. Most important, soapstone can be heated to be very hot, and unlike most stones, it won't crack. These characteristics together made it ideal for use as material for cooking vessels and smoking pipes.

At first, they mainly used the soapstone to make cooking stones. These were usually hand-sized pieces of soapstone with a hole carved out of the middle. To cook with it, a person would collect some water with other foods or herbs to make a stew in a small pit in the ground. The pit may have been lined with an animal skin or intestine to hold the water while the stone was heated in a fire. Once the stone was hot, a stick was poked through the hole to pick it up and put it into the water and heat up the stew. In addition to cooking stones, soapstone was later carved by archaic people to make atlatl weights, smoking pipes, gaming stones, ornaments and bowls of many shapes and sizes.

Soon they also discovered that the best source of soapstone in the Southeast is at the headwaters of the south fork of the Ocmulgee River (the South River), the area we now know as Atlanta. Many people settled around this resource and built the area's first permanent residences four thousand years ago. They created the first major manufacturing and trading zone in the history of the Atlanta area. Slabs of soapstone from prehistoric Atlanta were traded widely throughout the Southeast as far as Louisiana and even to the Great Lakes.

Many of these ancient soapstone quarries remain intact today and can be easily visited. One of the best is a quarry in Fork Creek Mountain Park. Visiting this little public park, you can take a walk through the woods behind the playground and peruse the handiwork of people who lived in the area four thousand years ago; there is stone still lying out on the ground as if the masons have just walked away from their work.

The most common relics you'll see at one of these quarries are large round carvings in the boulders. These are the remnants of the soapstone bowl making process. The mason would first locate a convenient bulge in the rocks suitable to become the underside of a bowl. They would then begin to carve out the base. The mason would then continue chipping away at the bulge until it resembled a sort of mushroom shape. They would then wedge branches into the gap to snap it away from the main rock and create a preform. The removal of the preform from the boulder would leave a rounded-out spot called a bowl scar. These bowl scars are still easily identified in these ancient quarries. Working a preform into an actual bowl would take around twenty hours of labor. These soapstone bowls were prized community possessions. They were heavy but would be carried from one living site to another for many years and were often placed with the deceased in burial sites.

This boulder in a public park near Atlanta shows clear signs of bowl making by the area's first residents perhaps five thousand years ago. *Photo by the author.*

The use of pottery arrived in Georgia at the coast about five thousand years ago and gradually took over the soapstone bowl trading business. The soapstone was still used to make ornamentation, and it continued to be the preferred material for making smoking pipes all the way through the colonial period. There were still people frequenting the quarries in the Atlanta area, but most of their homes shifted to be closer to the major creeks and rivers during the next two thousand years (from 1000 BC to AD 1000).

Generally, prehistoric Atlanta's natives spread out more and settled into areas along all of its major waterways. Bigger villages began to support fifty people or so. Living sites of this age have been located along the North Fork and the South Fork of Peachtree Creek, Snapfinger Creek, Sugar Creek and the South River. They are most common in the delta where two creeks or a creek and a river reach a confluence, such as the point where Peachtree Creek joins with the Chattahoochee River (where the settlement of Standing Peachtree/Pakanahuili was later built). The largest concentration of small camps and villages has been found along each fork of Peachtree Creek. There were also several small settlements in the Redan area along Barbashela Creek and Snapfinger Creek. Prehistoric people also inhabited at least five separate campsites spread across eight thousand acres along Stone Mountain Creek.

For the rest of the time before the arrival of Europeans around 1513, the culture of the native people of the area that would become Atlanta flourished. Native society reached its peak in terms of religion, art and customs. They fully turned to a town-based, agricultural way of life and prospered as a result.

Villages in the Atlanta area were organized into a chiefdom with other villages along the Chattachoochee River, probably associated with the village containing the Etowah mounds near Cartersville, Georgia. This and the other scattered villages up and down the river may have represented a total population of fifteen thousand people. People were also still residing along the north banks of the South River between 1,700 and 1,500 years ago.

There is a good likelihood that the main village of this chiefdom was very close to present-day Atlanta. There was a large mound village located where the Six Flags Over Georgia amusement park is now on the banks of the Chattahoochee River. This village contained several mounds and predated the better-known Etowah mound village near Cartersville by around eight hundred years. The oldest mounds at the Etowah site date back to around AD 1000, whereas the oldest portions of the site beneath Six Flags Over Georgia date to AD 200. The area around Six Flags also became the location of Sandtown, a historically important native town to the area. The Six Flags site was tragically bulldozed when the Great Southwest Development Corporation built the amusement park in 1967 before the mounds were ever studied. We lost vast amounts of information about an important site in Atlanta's prehistory.

Apart from the sites in the vicinity of Six Flags Over Georgia associated with the later village of Sandtown, there was another important ancient village containing mounds and other structures at the site of the old village of Standing Peachtree, where the Atlanta Waterworks pumping station is now located. Standing Peachtree was first occupied around AD 1000 and was occupied well into the nineteenth century, probably all the way up to Creek Removal and the Cherokee Trail of Tears.

The mounds and the chiefs that stood atop them were at the core of native culture before European arrival. To call these structure "mounds" makes them sound as if they are burial mounds or cairns. They are much more. Photos don't do them justice. Standing in front of one feels much more like you're visiting a pyramid than something someone would call a mound. Some of them are over ten stories high. There is no question you are looking at a very important structure that took a long time to build. To think they were built by hand, one load of dirt after another, without even the use of any horses or wheelbarrows, is incredible.

To the people who built them, the mounds represented the navel of the Earth itself, and the chief standing atop the mound was a representative of their central deity, the Sun. Looking up at the chief, the people felt and saw the dominance he commanded over the Earth. The chief was revered as a direct connection to the spiritual world—not a military leader. He performed rituals that changed the inner workings of the Earth and kept the tribe safe. He could ensure the rising of the sun, the warming of springtime and the periodic flooding of the river to soak the crops.

3

DECATUR'S CANNON AND THE NATIVE APOCALYPSE IN GEORGIA

In Decatur, the little city inside Atlanta's perimeter I-285 and six miles east of the city center of Atlanta, there is a little cannon mounted outside the old courthouse. It is inscribed with the phrase "Relic of the Indian War of 1836." The little cannon is not well known to most Atlantans and there is no plaque nearby describing it, but it played as critical a role in the founding of the city as any other relic of its history.

The story of how the little cannon became a part of local history began when the first Europeans made contact around 1513 to trade with the indigenous people they found. This was twenty-seven years before when most people think first contact was made in Georgia during Hernando de Soto's famous march through the interior of Georgia. By 1540, the results of that initial contact had devastating effects across Georgia and the rest of the Southeast. In the aftermath of the Creek War of 1836 where the little cannon saw action, every Creek Indian in Georgia was either killed or banished. By 1840, nearly every Cherokee and every other Native American was gone from the state.

The first and most deadly rider of this apocalypse for the natives of Georgia was disease. The Indians had lived for thousands of years completely isolated from Europe. As a result, they had not developed natural immunities to many of the common diseases introduced by the Europeans mainly through the domestic animals they brought with them.

This little cannon was a central element to many eras of Atlanta history from the conflicts with Native Americans to its antebellum riots. *Photo by the author.*

Certainly, more than half and conceivably as much as 90 percent of the native population perished from diseases like measles, smallpox and cholera that were brought by the Europeans. The few survivors of towns that were infected went to live with connected groups and accelerated the spread of these new diseases.

During Hernando de Soto's early trek through Georgia, as the first person to reach the interior of the Southeast in 1540, he made note of the growing devastation among the Indians: "The inhabitants are brown of skin, well-formed and proportioned. They are more civilized than any people in all the territories of Florida, wearing clothes and shoes. This country, according to what the Indians stated, had been very populous, but it had been decimated shortly before by a pestilence." Epidemics continued to cut through the Native American population from Georgia as late as 1783.

The second rider of the Indian apocalypse was in some ways even more tragic than the rampant deadly diseases because the Indians took an active role in creating their own misery. This was slavery. The Indians already practiced a form of slavery prior to European contact by capturing members of other groups who were forced to become slaves, but slaves were not bought and sold until the arrival of Europeans. This practice began with the Spanish and accelerated with the arrival of the British in the New World.

The European process for acquiring Indian slaves created a vicious cycle that greatly accelerated the already collapsing societal structure by which the Indians previously lived and kept balance with one another. This vicious cycle would start when a group of European traders agreed to give guns to a group of Indians on credit. That group of Indians would then use the guns to raid another group that had no guns and deliver their captives back to the traders as slaves to pay off their debt. Any Indians who had escaped among the enslaved group would then need to contact another group of traders to acquire more guns to defend themselves from further raids, and the primary way to get guns was to find another weaker group to prey upon for more slaves to deliver to the traders. And so it went. This cycle not only accelerated their own demise but also destroyed any hope the Indians would have of confronting the Europeans on equal ground as a unified nation.

Traders from Jamestown supported slave raids by Indians across most of the Piedmont. The Iroquois in the Northeast were some of the first Indians to take part in the slave trade for the British in Carolina during the early part of the 1600s. By the late 1600s, these slave raids had arrived in the Southeast. Iroquois raids from the north reached into current regions of Alabama, Georgia, Tennessee, Florida, Kentucky, Arkansas and Louisiana.

In response, there was a general migration of Indians in Georgia out of the mountains and down to the south and west toward Sandtown and Standing Peachtree (the area of the future Atlanta) on the Chattahoochee, and away from the Iroquois.

The last rider of the native apocalypse was commerce. As more and more Europeans found their way to America, the primary livelihood of most southeastern Indians shifted from subsistence hunting and farming to commercial hunting and slave trading. Other professions emerged for Indians that hadn't existed before like guide, translator, postal rider or hired soldier as well as horse thief, prostitute or slave catcher. This shift to commercial hunting and trading also led to the decimation of the white-tailed deer population in the South and the eventual shift of American and European interests from deerskins to farming.

The remaining native, cultural artifacts of early eighteenth-century Georgia have all the signs of a cultural collapse. Mound building stopped entirely. The creation of art and religious or ritualistic material completely disappeared. The intricate items with which people had been buried in past years were gone.

To gather together their remaining strength to both protect themselves and weaken other groups, the remaining Indian populations joined into loosely allied groups that are often collectively referred to as the "coalescent groups." There were many of these coalescent groups. Some of the larger and better known of them included the Creeks, the Cherokees, the Catawbas, the Chickasaw, the Apalachee, the Timucua, the Yamasee and the Seminoles. The primary groups that eventually encountered the new Europeans in Georgia were the Creeks and the Cherokees.

The term *coalescent group* is an accurate and important one because it conveys the point that these were not quite unique individual tribes, though they are often referred to using that term. They were collections of many different groups who agreed to act together as a unit to draw strength. Most accurately in the case of the Creeks, they are called a confederacy. Each of the groups that joined the coalescent groups or the Creek Confederacy had a unique history and character. By no means did they always see eye to eye with the other groups with whom they had agreed to generally cooperate.

The social and political organization among these Creek groups is based on a hierarchy of towns. The major towns of the Creek Confederacy were their centers of political power. These towns were generally divided into two major groups. The Upper Creeks lived in towns along the Coosa and the Tallapoosa Rivers in Alabama. The Lower Creeks occupied major towns

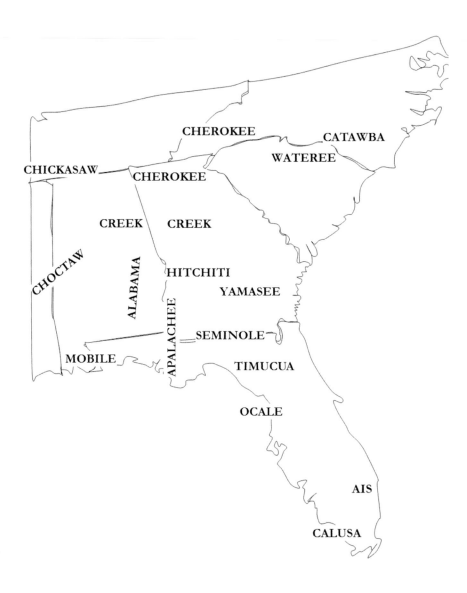

Approximate locations of the central coalescent native groups. *Sketch by the author using sources from University of California Irvine.*

along the Chattahoochee. The bigger Creek towns of the historical period included Autossee, Tuckabatchie, Muckfaw, Hoithlewallee, Chattahoochee, Wetumpka, Tallassee, Cussita and Coweta.

Over time, the Coweta became regarded as the undisputed leaders of the Lower Creeks and by some as the overall leaders of the Creek Confederacy. When the Americans began dealing with the Creeks later on, they viewed the Coweta as the primary leaders of the Creeks and looked to them to speak on behalf of the whole confederacy. This became a crucial area of disagreement among the Creeks and eventually led to tragedy.

The Coweta were also probably the first Creeks to ever make contact with Europeans. Not coincidentally, the rise in the power of the Coweta coincided with the time when the European contact was made. Their primary source of power was through trade with the English and later the Americans. This began with Henry Woodward in 1674. He was the first European trader to venture into the towns of the Creeks along the Chattahoochee to trade with them. He was also probably the first nonnative person to set foot in the future location of Atlanta. These stronger relationships with traders gave the Coweta greater power and influence than other Creeks.

Under these conditions, the Creeks and the Europeans met on equal ground for a short period of time. Each tried to get an advantage over the other and believed they had the greater negotiating power in the relationship. By 1704, the colonial Carolina and Virginia traders had created a thriving network with all the Creeks along the Chattahoochee. Commerce flowed fast and heavy through Five Points and the trails passing through the Atlanta area.

Various groups occupied the Atlanta area and then moved on over the millennia. At the time Europeans arrived, the two Creek towns near what would be Atlanta were called Sandtown and Standing Peachtree. Both were affiliated towns under the leadership of the major town of Coweta farther south on the Chattahoochee.

In addition to these two larger Creek villages near the future location of Atlanta, there were smaller villages called Kennesaw Town and Noonday Town, both near Noonsday Creek; Sweetwater Town, near the creek of that name; and Buffalo Fish Town, southeast of Marietta.

4

1,800 Years Before Atlanta, There Was Sandtown

Of the two Coweta towns in the Atlanta area, Sandtown and Standing Peachtree (Pakanahuili), Sandtown has the older history and probably ranked higher as a town among the Creeks than Standing Peachtree did. The limited archaeological work that has been done on Sandtown indicates it was a complex of a few different villages that were occupied at various times in history.

The first study of the area done in 1938 uncovered two human skeletons that had been interred in a highly ritualized burial. One of the skeletons found was seated upright, legs crossed, leaning against a stone slab, arms crossed at the wrists. An exact date of when these people were buried was never established.

At one time, there was a village that contained several mounds in the Sandtown area alongside the Chattahoochee. This was probably a very high-ranking town among the people of this period before the Creeks and may have contained a wealth of historical knowledge. Unfortunately, we will never know the exact age of this site or what it contained because it was destroyed when Six Flags Over Georgia was constructed in 1967 and never studied.

After the site was destroyed, a dig was funded at the historic town of Sandtown on the east bank of the Chattahoochee just north of Utoy Creek. The initial investigations of this site uncovered yet another, more pristine and much older site than Sandtown on the other side of Utoy Creek. This site, dubbed 9FU14, was found to date to around AD 300. It was a village

Aerial view of the Chattahoochee River at the location of the Creek village of Sandtown. *Photo by the author.*

of twenty-five structures—all houses, except for one much larger one at the middle of the village that that was probably a ceremonial dwelling. A similar site was excavated nearby on the grounds of Pebblebrook High School a little farther north.

Most of the known history of Sandtown took place during the years that Americans were interacting with the Creeks, from the late eighteenth century to Creek Removal in the late 1830s. At some point during the rise of the Coweta during the late sixteenth century, Sandtown became an expansion town of Coweta Town farther down the Chattahoochee. The Creeks revered the older towns and structures from the people who had come before and probably chose Sandtown as the location of an expansion town of Coweta out of reverence to the older mounds that were there.

At some point, perhaps in the early 1800s, the name Buzzard's Roost also became interchangeable with Sandtown. This name persists as the name of an island in the Chattahoochee at this location today.

By the mid-1700s, the Cherokees were arriving in the area that is now DeKalb County, pushed down by other predatory groups like the Iroquois and the Westos to the north and other slave raiding tribes to the east around Savannah. There was a general migration of Indians in Georgia toward the south. The Creeks local to the area assembled in the later incarnation of Sandtown around 1800 as the Cherokees took over Standing Peachtree.

After the founding of Decatur in 1823 and before the Creek Removal around 1836, Sandtown remained a well-established Creek town and was very familiar to the Georgia settlers. Indians from Sandtown frequently visited Decatur to trade and often passed through Five Points.

Vestiges of the original Sandtown can still be found along Campbellton Road in Southwest Atlanta. Even today, there is a community near the intersection of Campbellton Road and Camp Creek Parkway that is still called Sandtown.

5

STANDING PEACHTREE, THE OTHER NATIVE TOWN NORTH OF SANDTOWN

J ust upriver from Sandtown was the connected village of Standing Peachtree at the confluence of Peachtree Creek and the Chattahoochee River. Among the Creeks, it was known by the name Pakanahuili. It's better known to general history than Sandtown for several reasons. Chief among these reasons is that it gave us the names of several streets in Atlanta and its main roads. The oldest and most central to Atlanta, Peachtree Street, was so named because it was the path that led out of Five Points to Standing Peachtree. Second, Standing Peachtree came to be occupied by the Cherokees later in its history. The Cherokees stayed in the area longer than the Creeks did and were generally more friendly with the Americans than the Creeks were. As a result, the history of their interactions with the settlers is better documented. Third, the Americans built a fort there, resulting in more eyewitness accounts and references to Standing Peachtree and Fort Peachtree/Fort Gilmer than to Sandtown.

Like Sandtown, there appear to have been several periods of occupation in Standing Peachtree. Also, like Sandtown, the first of these occupations was over one thousand years ago. Carbon dating indicates the area was first occupied between 1034 and 1154, almost four hundred years before the first Spanish set foot in North America.

There were mound structures in and around the Standing Peachtree area reflecting that it was part of a very old chiefdom, probably associated with the older village that was in the Sandtown location. This location was probably chosen by the Coweta to revere the older structures when they

The north bank between Peachtree Creek and the Chattahoochee River was the location of the Creek and later Cherokee village of Standing Peachtree. *Photo by the author.*

expanded out of Coweta town into the area that would become Atlanta at some point prior to the Revolutionary War.

The origin of the name Standing Peachtree is an often-discussed topic among people interested in Atlanta's history because it became the source of so many more names throughout the city. There are at least two plausible stories regarding the possible origin of the name. One commonly recited story is that there was an enormous pine tree on the bank near the creek that was blazed so that the local Indians could gather sap—also called pitch— from it. Hence, it was the pitch tree.

The more likely of the stories is that it was named for an actual peach tree that stood on top of the enormous mound at that location. Peaches were initially brought to America by the Spanish in the mid-sixteenth century. So, it's theoretically possible one made its way to the Atlanta area this far back.

Most people tend to believe the pitch tree story as more plausible than a fruit tree having existed on Atlanta's riverbanks so long ago. As surprising as it is, the fact is we have a credible witness to the story about the peach tree. George Washington Collier, one of Atlanta's earliest residents, carried the mail between Decatur and Allatoona in the 1830s. He passed by the old fort and Standing Peachtree often in his mail deliveries and attested to the fact that there was indeed a large, old peach tree growing there.

> *This is the way it was: Standing Peachtree post office was right where Peachtree Creek runs into the Chattahoochee—right where the pumping station is now. It was not Peachtree Creek then—they called it some Indian name. There was a great, huge mound of earth heaped up there—big as this house, maybe bigger, right on top of it grew a big peach tree. It bore fruit and was a useful and beautiful tree.*
> *—George Washington Collier*

Case closed.

The first known mention of the location as Standing Peachtree comes from a letter written on May 27, 1782, by John Marten to General Andrew Pickens. It also makes mention of William McIntosh, the leader of the Coweta who figured prominently in Atlanta's prehistory. This letter may have concerned the Oconee War in the late 1780s and early 1790s.

Standing Peachtree also appeared in a note written later that year in August. The note was used to make a payment to John Brandon for his "secret service" in traveling to Standing Peachtree to meet with the Indians there. This was probably a trip made to secure the support or neutrality of the Indians living there in some military task having to do with the Revolutionary War or to try to strengthen the relationships with the Creeks in preparation for the establishment of the new United States.

1782 LETTER REGARDING STANDING PEACHTREE

May 27, 1782
Dear Genl:

> *I have just had the pleasure of seeing our good firm and fast friend the Tallasee King, who has come down with a Talk to me and has brought about forty of his head Men and Warriors with him.*
> *He informs me, that Mr. McIntosh with a strong party of the Coweta, etc. were to rendezvous at the Standing Peach Tree the 26ᵗʰ of this month and they were afterwards to meet at the Big Shoal where they were to meet*

a number of Cherokees after which they were to fall on the Okonnys [sic]
on our Frontiers, therefore we have every reason to expect that they will be
in upon our back Settlements in about 8 or 10 days at the farthest. I doubt
not my der [sic] *Genl., you will take proper measures and endeavor to give*
us every and the most early assistance in your power—for God's sake exert
yourself and come in to our timely aid, as delays are dangerous. I have
wrote [sic] *to Col. Clarke on this matter who I dare say will be happy to*
see you—In the meantime I am

Dr. Genl. Your Most Obt. Sert.
JNO Martin
Copy
The Honble. Genl. Pickins [sic]
So. Carolina

There is no further information available about the actual incident discussed and whether McIntosh met with General Pickens. Tallassee King, known as Hopoithle Mico among the Creeks, was another of the Creek chiefs who participated in several treaties with the British and the Americans. He would eventually take part in the Red Stick War on the side of the Red Sticks fighting the Americans and their Lower Creek allies. He died in November 1813 in the battle at Calebee Creek, Alabama.

One of the earliest settlers in the Atlanta area who came to be closely associated with Standing Peachtree was James McConnell Montgomery. He took up his first of a few residencies in the area in 1814. In response to unrest among the Creeks during the early nineteenth century, the U.S. government established a series of forts stringing together strategic locations in the frontier. These forts were intended to establish a supply line from General Pinkney at Charleston, South Carolina, south to Brigadier General Floyd at Fort Mitchell at the Falls of the Chattahoochee and then General Jackson at Columbus, Georgia. One of these stops in the supply line was intended to be Fort Peachtree at Standing Peachtree. Another was placed at Hog Mountain in Gwinnett County.

Young James McConnell Montgomery was put under the command of George Rockingham Gilmer with twenty-one other soldiers to establish the fort and put it in order as a boatyard and supply stop on the Chattahoochee River. He had no idea at that time of the deep effects Standing Peachtree would have on the rest of his life.

According to Gilmer, as a detachment of soldiers, they were lightly equipped, having only "a lot of flintlocks that nobody else wanted that had seen more service at the annual musters than at the firing line" and "some loose powder and a small quantity of unmolded lead for bullets."

They built a compound consisting of a large log blockhouse, six dwellings and a storehouse on the east side of the river opposite the creek. The fort was placed on the north side of Peachtree Creek and the boatyard on the south bank of the creek. They also built a bridge half a mile from the fort.

There were two minor incidents where the troops at Fort Peachtree were called into soldierly duty. In the first case, some Cherokees came to the soldiers one night to inform them that a group of Creek warriors were on their way to attack the fort. Preparations were made, and the soldiers lay in trenches ready for an attack that never came. The incident was probably fabricated by the Cherokees as an attempt to persuade the soldiers to abandon the area.

The second incident was a result of the American victory of Andrew Jackson over the Red Stick Creeks in the Battle of Horseshoe Bend. Captain Gilmer heard gunshots in the village of Standing Peachtree and called his soldiers to arms from their work cutting trees in the woods for lumber. As it turned out, the gunshots were a celebration by the Cherokees who had returned from the battle with eighteen scalps that they were parading door to door on a pole.

Overall, the establishment of the supply stop at Fort Peachtree was a failure. Only five of the intended ten boats were built, and these failed to stand up to the Chattahoochee's shoals and fell apart. The efforts at creating a boatyard were abandoned in May 1814 after just a few months of effort.

6

CIVIL WAR INSIDE
THE CREEK NATION

Within the Creek Confederacy, there were two opposing views on how to deal with the Americans that reflected the mirror image of the opposing American views. In general, the Lower Creeks favored much more open relationships with the Americans, while the Upper Creeks favored isolation. The supporters of each view had grown more divided to the point the two sections of the overall confederacy, the Upper Creeks and the Lower Creeks, operated in many ways like two strong political parties. Each tried to sway the Creek National Council to its point of view.

This general policy disagreement became a serious power struggle that divided the Creek Confederacy around 1800 after the death of one of its great chiefs, Alexander McGillvray, and the decline of English trading in America.

As the Creeks felt their power waning and settlers continued to intrude illegally on Creek land in greater and greater numbers with no opposition from the state governments, the Upper Creeks were becoming demoralized. The loss of all Creek land seemed increasingly unavoidable. They were becoming desperate for a new vision of hope, and in 1811, Tecumseh, the famous Shawnee warrior, brought it to them.

In 1811, Tecumseh came to visit the Creek National Council with a vision that had been articulated by his brother Tenskwatawa, a renowned Shawnee prophet. The Creeks considered the Shawnees to be people of the "same fireside," having emerged from the same ancestors. Tecumseh was well known and respected by the Creeks and was considered a Creek by some, his mother being a Creek from one of the Upper Towns. Tecumseh gave a fiery and inspiring speech before the Creek Council appealing to their frustrations and outrage at the power of the Americans. He painted visions of how all Indians would join in a united force that would push the Americans back into the sea. Then, they would rid the land of all things American and return to a traditional Indian culture. Tecumseh's call to arms was taken down by the famous frontiersman Sam Dale, who was present:

> *Accursed be the race that has seized on our country and made women of our warriors. Our fathers, from their tombs, reproach us as slaves and cowards. I hear them now in the wailing winds. The Muscogee was once a mighty people. The Georgians trembled at your war whoop, and the maidens of my tribe, on the distant lakes, sung the prowess of your warriors and sighed for their embraces. Now your very blood is white; your tomahawks have no edge; your bows and arrows were buried with your fathers. Oh! Muscogees! Brethren of my mother! Brush from your eyelids the sleep of slavery; once more strike for vengeance—once more for your country. The spirits of the mighty dead complain! Their tears drop from the weeping skies! Let the white race perish! They seize your land; they corrupt your women; they trample on the ashes of your dead! Back! Whence they came! Upon a trail of blood, they must be driven! Back! Back, ay, into the great water whose, accursed waves brought them to our shorts! Burn their dwellings! Destroy their stock! Slay their wives and children! The Red Man owns the country, and the palefaces must never enjoy it! War now! War forever! War upon the living! War upon the dead! Dig their very corpses from the grave! Our country must give no rest to a white man's bones!*

After the Shawnees' visit, several of the Creek leaders traveled to the Great Lakes to meet with other followers of Tenskwatawa. They returned with more inspiring rhetoric and promises. Tenskwatawa's followers had taught them sacred rituals and dances to their deity Hisagati Misi, "The Master of Breath," that they believed would shield them from American bullets and cannon fire. In addition, they promised that Tecumseh's warriors and their old allies the British were gathering and would soon come to support them.

Tecumseh masterfully intertwined his brother's vision and the frustration of all Indians with the brewing War of 1812 between the British and the Americans into his own vision for a united Indian nation. The National Council never officially agreed to put the support of the Creeks behind

Tecumseh, but it didn't matter. The majority of Upper Creeks leapt to support the vision anyway.

When a Creek town went to war, there was a tradition to declare this by hanging a stick colored red, their traditional color for war, in the town square. Thus the followers of this movement became known as the Red Sticks.

The wrath of the Red Sticks was as much focused on other Creeks as it was the Americans. They believed that the Creeks who favored compromise and negotiation with the Americans had sold away their culture and their power in the New World. In general, the Upper Creeks tended to support the Red Stick movement while the Lower Creeks supported continued relationships with the Americans, but this was not at all absolute. Some Creek towns were divided against each other, and many people from each region left to join the other side. In addition, many Indians who were not Creek chose to join the Red Sticks.

The Red Sticks' first efforts were to purge themselves of anything they viewed as an American influence. They destroyed Creek farms. They threw plows and looms into the river. They slaughtered any farm animals they found among the Creeks.

In the spring of 1813, a group of the Red Sticks traveled to Pensacola to gather supplies from the British trading house there. They were probably inspired by British soldiers who supplied them with weapons through Panton, Leslie and Company to destabilize the Americans in the Southeast. On their way back, they were attacked by a group of Mississippi militia led in part by Lower Creek headmen from the Tensaw and Bigbe settlements just north of Pensacola. In retaliation, on August 29, 1813, the Red Sticks attacked and defeated the garrison at Fort Mims near present-day Mobile, Alabama. They killed nearly every settler and Lower Creek Indian living there.

The Red Stick War had begun.

Over the following weeks, several quickly assembled armies from Mississippi, Georgia and Tennessee took to the field supported by their Indian allies from the Choctaws, Cherokees and Lower Creeks in the Red Stick War. They were led by Andrew Jackson, the commander of the Tennessee Militia, who called for a "spirit of revenge" to annihilate the Red Sticks. In English, the Red Sticks named him "Mad Dog" Jackson.

The British were highly suspected of having supplied the Creeks with weapons but never deployed any forces to support them. The Americans were successful in putting the Creeks on the run and winning a series of battles. American soldiers marveled at the Red Sticks doing their dances to the Master of Breath in front of the cannons with the expectation that they wouldn't be harmed. However, none of these battles was definitive enough to crush the Red Stick forces. Most of the Creeks were able to escape each confrontation and reassemble in another location. They were still a potent and dangerous threat to the Americans.

By the spring of 1814, Andrew Jackson's army was the only one still active in the field, and the bulk of the remaining Red Stick forces were assembled near the town of Tohopeka. As the Americans pursued them, the Red Sticks made careful preparations to meet the Americans and decide the war. Each knew this would be the battle to decide the Red Stick War. The Red Sticks believed they had gathered a much larger force than the Americans and were determined to execute this battle differently from the sprawling town battles they had made in the past.

The face-off between the Americans and the Red Sticks was not the only major confrontation taking place at Horseshoe Bend. The Upper Creeks and their greatest leaders were going to meet the leader of the Lower Creeks face to face, and the civil war within the Creek Confederacy would also be decided.

On one side, leading the Red Sticks, was Menawa "Hothlepoya," the great war hunter, the legendary second chief from the powerful Creek town of Oakfuskee. It is not certain in which battles Menawa participated before the Battle of Horseshoe Bend. There were probably several. He may have fought with his kindred the Oakfuskee at Autossee, the Creek encampment of Emuckfau (also called Muckfaw Town) and the previous battle with Jackson's forces at Enitichopco Creek.

On the opposite side of the conflict fighting with the Americans was William McIntosh, the war leader of the Lower Creeks. McIntosh embodied all of the hopes of the Lower Creeks for assimilation into the United States. He was an influential Creek with a good education and some status among the Americans. McIntosh was even connected by family bonds to many Americans in government, including his cousin (second cousin once removed) George Troup, the governor of Georgia at that time, and Lachlan McIntosh, the general who commanded the Continental Troops in Georgia during much of the Revolutionary War.

McIntosh was a Coweta, one of the major towns on the Chattahoochee affiliated with Sandtown. He led around two hundred Lower Creeks into the Battle of Horseshoe Bend. The Atlanta area was well represented at the Battle of Horseshoe Bend. There were probably some braves from Sandtown under McInstosh's command. Jackson also commanded a group of Cherokees, including some from Standing Peachtree.

Menawa and McIntosh knew each other well. Their rivalry for leadership within the Creek Nation had already been growing for many years. Years before the Battle of Horseshoe Bend, one of the Upper Creek villages was burned in retribution for the murder of an American settler. Some said the murder was committed by Menawa's band. Menawa vehemently denied the rumors. He believed those false reports were delivered by McIntosh, whom he thought to be the real culprit of the murder in a scheme to play the Americans against him and further solidify McIntosh's own position as the primary Creek leader.

The Red Sticks chose a spot where there is a sharp 180-degree bend in the Tallapoosa River near Tohopeka to make their stand. They had gathered around one thousand Red Stick warriors and converted the bend of the river into a fortress. The river served as a natural moat at the back and on the sides. In front, where an army could approach on land, the Red Sticks dug out trenches and built up a barricade of logs with openings from which they could fire their weapons. Menawa oversaw much of the preparations. They did a masterful job choosing a location and fortifying it, which Jackson praised many times in descriptions of the battle:

> It is impossible to conceive of a situation more eligible for defence than the one they had chosen and the skill they manifested in their breastwork was really astonishing. It was from five to eight feet high and extended across the point in such a direction as that a force approaching would be exposed to a double fire, while they lay entirely safe behind it. It would have been impossible to have raked it with cannon to any advantage even if we had had possession of one extremity.

Despite the Red Sticks' excellent preparations at the front of the attack, they knowingly left themselves vulnerable at the back, where there was a small village containing women and children. During their preparations making Horseshoe Bend into a barricade, the first chief of the Oakfuskee whom Menawa followed declared that he had learned through supernatural means that the attack would come from the thin opening of land in the horseshoe, not from across the river at the rear. His followers believed him and put all their efforts into fortifying this side of the bend.

On the morning of March 27, 1814, a day before the battle, Jackson made probably his most important maneuver by splitting his force in two. He sent General Coffee ahead at 6:30 a.m. with the mounted Americans and most of the Indians, a force of seven hundred cavalry and mounted horsemen and about six hundred Indian allies. The Indian forces consisted of around four hundred Cherokees and William McIntosh with his two hundred or so Lower Creeks.

Jackson did not plan to just win this battle. His objective was to exterminate the whole of the Indian force. Therefore, he wanted Coffee and his Cherokee and Lower Creek forces to "surround the bend in such a manner, as that none of them should escape by attempting to cross the river" Sometime during the morning of March 28, General Coffee sent McIntosh and most of the other Indians ahead of the American troops with orders to position themselves at the rear of the battleground across the river and behind the Red Stick's barricade.

Around the time Coffee was approaching the battleground with his horses, about ten o'clock in the morning, Jackson was approaching the barricade from the front with his force of around two thousand regular soldiers and militia and two cannons. Upon sighting them, Coffee recalled that "a savage yell was raised" by the Indians in the barricade that must have bristled the hair on backs of the necks of the American forces.

Jackson placed his two cannons (a six-pounder and a three-pounder) on a small hill around 150 to 200 yards from the front of the barricade. The battle began quickly and in earnest with the firing of the cannons into the front of the Red Sticks' fortifications. The American forces supported the cannon fire with their rifles in both the front and the rear.

As the battle opened, the Indians in the village who weren't part of the fighting began running for cover in a panic but were prevented from approaching the river by Coffee, McIntosh and the Indians on the opposite bank firing across at them. The cannon balls failed to break the front of the barricade as Jackson had intended, but many of them passed through and ripped apart any Red Stick warriors unlucky enough to be in their path.

The next hours were the bloodiest and most brutal of all the engagements between the Creeks and the Americans. The Red Sticks knew this would be the day that decided whether they would continue as a people in the Southeast. Some of them still believed they were protected by the rituals the Shawnee had taught them. They fought with the desperation that comes when there is no option for retreat.

Jackson described the action, saying that each side "maintained for a few minutes a very obstinate contest, muzzle to muzzle, through the port-holes, in which many of the enemy's balls were welded to the bayonets of our musquets." (They stuck their bayonets down the muzzle of the rifles protruding from the barricade, thereby plugging them as the Indians fired.)

The American forces kept up this assault on both sides for the next two hours or so with a few brief interruptions. Around midday, several of the Indians at the rear under Coffee's command broke away from the line at the riverbank and dove into the river to cross over into the village. Some of them grabbed canoes that were resting on the bank behind the village and began to ferry their comrades across. Others proceeded into the village, setting it on fire and advancing to the back of the barricade. The Creeks and Cherokees had disobeyed Coffee's orders to make this move, but it became the main turning point in the battle.

Sensing that this was the moment the Red Sticks would fall, Jackson ordered a charge from the front while the barricade was being attacked from behind. Jackson later described his troops at this moment: "Never were men better disposed for such an undertaking than those by whom it was to be effected. They had entreated to be lead [*sic*] to the charge with the most pressing importunity and received the order which was now given with the strongest demonstration of joy."

Inside the barricade, Menawa realized the Red Sticks were being viciously attacked from the rear and the village had been set afire despite their false faith in the first chief's prophecy that the attack would come only from the direction of the barricade. Amid the chaos, he took a small group of warriors and ran through the battle to find the first chief of the Oakfuskee and slew him on the spot. Then, he gathered his closest Red Stick warriors about him and went to meet the Americans who were now storming over the barricade at the front. Menawa and his warriors waded into their midst battling hand-to-hand and muzzle-to-muzzle.

Among those who stormed over the barricade in Jackson's infantry was another well-known figure to later history. A young third lieutenant named Sam Houston was wounded twice during the Battle of Horseshoe Bend.

The entire battle lasted about five hours. The killing continued through the night and into the next day. In the morning, the riverbank was strewn with the dead. The Americans counted 557 Red Sticks lying dead on the bank and estimated that another few hundred were killed and had been swept under by the Tallapoosa. They had taken 250 Indians prisoner. All but 3 of these were women and children.

Most of the dead were killed by General Coffee and his men as they tried to escape out the rear of the barricade. Jackson estimated that no more than 20 Red Stick warriors escaped alive; 16 more Red Sticks were killed

Jackson's Tennessee Militia storms over the barricade at the battle of Horseshoe Bend.
Illustrations by Chulsan Um.

the day after the battle when they were found hiding in the water under the riverbank. The army's final death count was 850 Red Sticks. Among Jackson's force, there were 25 killed and 106 wounded.

According to the Red Sticks in later accounts, the number who escaped was closer to seventy warriors of the thousand who had been in the battle. Three of the Red Sticks' principal leaders were killed in the battle, including the first chief of the Oakfuskee slain by Menawa and another chief named Monashee who had spoken strongly and convincingly against the Americans. Jackson took pleasure in noting in one of his letters that Monashee had received a grapeshot to the mouth, thereby closing it for good. (Grapeshot are iron balls that are fired from a cannon in a bunch.) McIntosh showed himself well enough in the battle to get a mention in one of Jackson's accounts: "Major McIntosh, (the Cowetau) [*sic*] who joined my army with a part of his tribe, greatly distinguished himself."

Amazingly, Menawa, though he fought viciously in the thick of the battle, survived the ordeal. Meeting the Americans face-to-face as they stormed over the barricade, Menawa was wounded by seven balls before he finally fell to the ground. He awoke several hours later, bleeding profusely, yet still clutching his gun to his chest. The bulk of the action had ceased, and the light of day was fading when he awoke. He still heard intermittent shots being fired. He slowly rose to a sitting position and was confronted by a soldier who was inspecting the dead. Each man raised his rifle, and the two fired almost simultaneously. Menawa killed the soldier but received another wound as the bullet passed through his cheek near the ear and out the other side of his face, taking several of his teeth. He fell back unconscious once again but remained alive. He could feel the Americans walking over his body as they continued to search among the dead and full night fell.

He awoke later after full darkness, feeling somewhat revived. He crawled over the bodies to the riverbank and found a canoe there that he quietly entered. By rolling side to side while lying on the bottom, he slowly dislodged it from the bank and floated silently downriver. The canoe eventually reached the swamp at Elkahatchee, where several women and children had been waiting since before the battle. Seeing the canoe approach, they pulled it to the shore and found their mangled chief lying unconscious in the bottom, barely alive.

Menawa was brought to a rendezvous point in the swamp where the survivors of the battle had chosen to meet should things go awry. For the next three days, the surviving Red Sticks held a secret council where they considered what to do next. After three days, it was decided that each of them would return home and admit defeat. All of them surrendered to the Americans except Menawa, who was still too badly wounded to travel. When Menawa was finally able, he returned home to a cold greeting in Oakfuskee. His village had been burned to the ground. Everything he owned had been taken away.

Menawa never returned to Horseshoe Bend on the Tallapoosa. It was said that he believed it to be haunted. Undoubtedly, he was indeed haunted by his memories of the place.

The Creeks were then forced to sign the Treaty of Fort Jackson in 1814, ending the Red Stick War. Benjamin Hawkins, the Creek agent, was there representing the federal government during the negotiations, but Andrew Jackson took over completely. Though he was supported by McIntosh and his Creeks in the war, Jackson was determined to remove any of the remaining power base of the entire Creek Confederacy. Upper Creeks and Lower Creeks together were forced to give up two-thirds of their remaining territory. Twenty-two million acres of Creek Land was ceded to the United States, including a huge tract of southern Georgia that was Lower Creek territory. The Creeks still had possession of most of the land west of the Ocmulgee River and in the northern parts of Georgia and Alabama.

Benjamin Hawkins protested before the signing of the Treaty that the border and the terms were too harsh and punished both factions of the Creeks even though many had supported the Americans against the Red Sticks. He was literally pushed aside from the table by Andrew Jackson. Not long after the signing of the Treaty of Fort Jackson, Hawkins submitted his resignation of his post as Creek agent on February 15, 1815. It was not accepted, and Hawkins served as the agent until his death the following June.

Jackson closed a letter to Major General Pinkney in 1814 with this: "The power of the Creeks is I think forever broken." And in this, he was largely correct. Most of the Upper Creek towns were now all destroyed. Their followers were scattered. Thousands of Red Stick followers fled Georgia to join the Seminoles to the south and continue resistance to the Americans. Others fled to Lower Creek towns like Coweta, where they admitted defeat and joined the Lower Creeks. Many others drifted back to Buzzard's Roost or Sandtown until they were all forcibly removed.

7

THE CREEKS GIVE ATLANTA LAND
TO GEORGIA

The Battle of Horseshoe Bend and the end of the Red Stick War didn't just take away the Creeks' land and power. It swayed American public sentiment against them. The federal policy of assimilation over expulsion was greatly weakened, while the state's case for expulsion had strengthened.

Despite more recent progress through the Treaty of Fort Jackson, Georgia was increasingly and openly critical of the federal government's progress in fulfilling the promise it had made in the Compact of 1802 to "extinguish the Indian title to all...lands within the state of Georgia." The president redoubled federal efforts to acquire land in Georgia. William McIntosh was the United States' primary ally in pushing forward a new round of agreements.

The land on which Atlanta is located was officially given over to the United States by the Creeks in Indian Springs, Georgia (the plantation owned by William McIntosh about fifty miles south of Atlanta), on January 8, 1821. The 1821 Treaty of Indian Springs sold half of the land remaining to the Lower Creeks over to the Americans, approximately 6,700 square miles, including the land that would become Atlanta. It included all the land between the Ocmulgee River and the Flint River and south of roughly where Alpharetta, Georgia, is now.

Under the terms of the agreement, the United States would pay the Creeks $10,000 at signing and $40,000 more when the treaty was ratified. The U.S. government would also pay a total of $200,000 in various annual

Portrait of the Coweta leader William McIntosh. *Library of Congress.*

payments over the next fourteen years. The parties also agreed that $250,000 would be paid by the federal government to Georgia claimants as restitution for stolen and damaged property. McIntosh was personally paid $40,000 for arranging the treaty.

The Creeks were also careful to keep control of Sandtown. It included a stipulation that if the boundary should "strike the Chattahoochee below the Creek village of Buzzard's Roost (Sandtown), there shall be a set aside

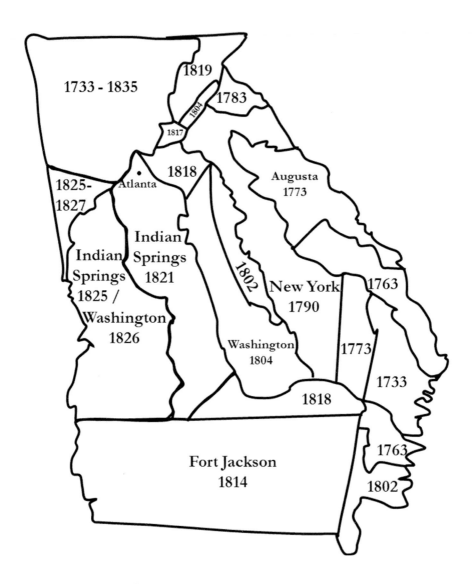

Map of the cessions of Georgia land from the Native Americans. *Sketch by the author using sources from University of Georgia.*

made to leave the village one mile within the Creek Nation." There were more carve-outs of land for the Creeks of 1,000 acres around Lock-Chau-talo-fau, a tract around the Creek agency that would be given to the United States when the agency was removed and 640 acres on the west bank of the Ocmulgee that belonged to Chief McIntosh.

This treaty was a dangerous one for McIntosh to orchestrate. He had overstepped. McIntosh should have gotten the full consent of the Creek National Council to sign this treaty. However, since the land that was given to the United States in the treaty of 1821 all belonged to the Lower Creeks and the two Creek leaders who had negotiated the treaty were the leaders of the Lower Creeks (McIntosh and Tustennuggee Hopoie), the National Council agreed to give its consent and the treaty was ratified. Now that nearly all the Creek land in Georgia belonged to the United States, the Creek National Council was adamant that no more land should be sold.

8

THE SECOND TREATY OF INDIAN SPRINGS AND THE COWETA CHIEF

In 1825, two agents of the federal government, Duncan G. Campbell and James Meriwether, were sent to the South to settle the Creek issue once and for all by procuring a final treaty that would give the remainder of Indian land in Georgia to the United States in exchange for money and land west of the Mississippi River on the Arkansas River. The two agents first visited Cherokees but were unsuccessful. They then visited the Creek National Council in 1825 to plead their case.

Menawa, after being nearly killed in the Battle of Horseshoe Bend, had reemerged as an influential force on the Creek National Council. After recovering from his injuries in the secret hiding place in the Elkahatchee swamp along the Tallapoosa and returning home to find his village burned, Menawa reassembled those who were left of the Oakfuskee and took his place on the council as their chief. He continued to oppose any attempts by the Americans to gain control of Creek lands.

Before the two agents were able to meet with the Creek National Council, a council mainly composed of Upper Creeks, met in Tuckabatchee in May 1824 and released a statement through the newspaper: "On deep and solemn reflection, we have, with one voice, [decided] to follow the pattern of the Cherokees, and on no account whatever will we consent to sell one foot of our land, neither by exchange or otherwise."

Nevertheless, a meeting was set in Broken Arrow with the agents and most of the National Council. When the two agents met with the council in December 1824 to propose a new treaty, Menawa was among many who vehemently opposed it. The resolution set in Tuckabatchee held. The agents were sent away with no agreement.

Still undeterred, the agents set a meeting with William McIntosh at his plantation in Indian Springs. They tried their best to achieve the same success the United States had just had with him in the treaty of 1821. A meeting was set calling the Creek chiefs to meet at Indian Springs. Very few of the Creeks from the Upper Towns attended.

Among the few Upper Creeks who attended was Hopoithle Yoholo, the second chief of Tuckabatchee, one of the more powerful towns. Once the proposal was laid out, this chief stood and said,

> *You asked us to sell you more lands at Broken Arrow; we told you we had none to spare. I told McIntosh then, that he knew no land could be sold except in full council and by consent of the nation. We have met here at a very short notice. Only a few chiefs are present from the upper towns and many are absent from the lower towns. That is all the talk I have to make, and I shall go home.*

With that, he departed.

McIntosh's confidence wavered. He was on the verge of calling off the meetings. The federal agents spoke with him in private, and upon their assurances that he would have the full protection of the United States, the meeting resumed.

The Second Treaty of Indian Springs was signed on February 12, 1825, by all those still present. The treaty gave all remaining Creek land in Georgia and east of Oakfuskee to the United States. McIntosh and his followers each received $200,000 right away, with further payments to occur once removal of the Creeks had begun. They each also received land in present-day Oklahoma, the location of the Creek Reservation. McIntosh was given permanent rights to his reserve on the Chattahoochee. The Indian Springs plantation was already reserved for him in the treaty of 1821. A phrase was added to the preamble of the treaty indicating the abstention of the chiefs from Tuckabatchee.

Among those who signed the treaty were three chiefs from Sandtown. These were Konope Emautla, Chawacala Mico and Foctalustee Emaulta. One of these chiefs, Chawacala Mico, signed the 1821 Treaty of Indian Springs, but his name is spelled Chaughle Micco on that treaty. As the Creeks had no written language, their names and titles had various spellings.

When it was first reported to them, the Creek National Council refused to believe that McIntosh and the other chiefs had signed a treaty that transferred the rest of the Creek land in Georgia to the Americans. When the report was then confirmed to be true by Crowell, the Creek agent at that time, the news went off like a bombshell. Crowell was in danger of losing his own life for having signed the treaty as a witness while knowing many of the chiefs opposed it. The role of the agent in the execution of the treaty became very suspicious in later years and is a subject of current study and debate.

According to the resolutions written in Tuckabatchee, if anyone signed a treaty on behalf of the Creeks without the consent of the National Council, "guns and ropes would be their end." The council convicted McIntosh and his close allies. They issued a death sentence for him as well as his family members and the other high-ranking chiefs of the Lower Creeks who had signed.

The chiefs of the Oakfuskee and Muckfaw Town and Tustennuggee Hopqui "Little Prince" took primary roles in convicting McIntosh and demanding the death sentence. Little Prince signed the 1821 Treaty of Indian Springs but not the 1825 treaty. Menawa, the great warrior of the Oakfuskee, was selected to see to the administration of the sentence. Somewhat surprisingly, Menawa at first refused and asked the council to choose someone who had less personal involvement in the matter to make it clear justice was being dealt out and not revenge. The council prevailed upon him, and Menawa agreed. He was soon leading a band of two hundred Oakfuskee, Talladega and Muckfaw braves toward Lock-Chau-talo-fau.

McIntosh was at his house in Lock-Chau-talo-fau with his family, a few fellow Coweta leaders and a few Americans. They were preparing to venture out to the west the following morning to inspect land to which McIntosh and many of the other Lower Creeks would soon be removing themselves out of Georgia.

Around two hundred Creek "Law Menders" arrived in Lock-Chau-talo-fau at dawn the morning of April 30, 1825. Along with them was one white man by the name of Hudman who was sent as an interpreter to make sure all present understood the reasoning in the charges. Once the Law Menders had surrounded McIntosh's house, Menawa called to those inside, "Let the white people who are in this house come out! And so, will the women and children! We come not to injure them! McIntosh has broken the law made by himself, and we have come to kill him for it!"

The Americans who were inside came out and were allowed to leave. Among them, McIntosh's son Chilly McIntosh and another Creek named

William Kennard slipped by unnoticed. Their names were also on the death warrant issued by the Creek National Council for having also signed the treaty, but each being younger and of mixed ancestry, they were able to pass themselves off as white children. Only two people remained in the house—William McIntosh and Eotmie Tustennuggee—the two Lower Creeks most responsible.

Menawa and his warriors set the house on fire. They then demanded that McIntosh come out and present himself before the Law Menders. They had a speech prepared and wanted to make the sentencing official. McIntosh refused to come out. Instead, he fired a rifle from the upper story. The shot only flashed though. No ball discharged.

All the Creeks surrounding the house then fired through the windows and doorway. McIntosh and Eotmie Tustennuggee came to the top of the staircase among the growing flames and were shot dead there on the steps by an immense volley of balls. McIntosh's body was dragged out into the yard and fired on several more times by the Law Menders. An enraged servant with no ears stepped forward and attacked the corpse with a knife as revenge for harsh punishment he was give because he stole from McIntosh. McIntosh was hit so many times that his body was said to have been "blown to pieces."

All of McIntosh's belongings that could be reached were then plundered. One of William McIntosh's three wives later went to the Upper Creek camp to reclaim their belongings. She came away with only a slave woman and her child. McIntosh and Eotmie Tustennuggee were buried nearby later that day.

Chilly McIntosh and William Kennard were spotted later that day and made a daring escape from a Creek patrol out looking for them. There were said to be several hundred more Creeks who had appeared in the area apart from the two hundred Law Menders. Several shots were fired at them, and at least one ball came close enough to shred Chilly McIntosh's shirt. They dove into a creek and hid in the banks of the Chattahoochee until that night. Chilly's sister brought them a canoe after nightfall, and they slid quietly across the river. Chilly survived the ordeal and eventually went to Oklahoma with the rest of the Creek Nation. He reemerged among the Creeks and became an important leader in the reformed Creek/Muscogee Nation there. Undoubtedly, this would have made his father proud.

At the same time the party of Law Menders appeared in Lock-Chau-talo-fau, two more parties were out looking for William McIntosh's son-in-law Benjamin Hawkins and his brother Samuel Hawkins. Benjamin was located about twenty-five miles away from Lock-Chau-talo-fau and brought back to

The death of William McIntosh and Etomme Tustennuggee in Lock-Chau-talo-fau.
Illustrations by Chulsan Um.

Muckfaw Town in Alabama. After appearing before the chiefs of Muckfaw Town, he was shot dead. Samuel Hawkins was spotted and shot, but he escaped and survived.

Though he hadn't sought it, it appeared that Menawa had the final revenge on McIntosh. The history that soon followed would show this to be a hollow and short-lived victory indeed.

In the wake of the disastrous Second Treaty of Indian Springs, the Creek chiefs, led by Menawa and Hopoithle Yoholo, the only Creek who left the negotiations for the treaty of 1825, went in another delegation to Washington to declare this treaty was unlawful. They were successful, at least at first. The U.S. government nullified the treaty on January 24, 1826, because it did not have the support of the National Council of Creeks.

In its place, the Treaty of Washington was negotiated. Realizing the inevitability of removal, the Creeks agreed to cede all Creek land to the United States except for three million acres in Alabama. The Creeks would retain all their land until January 1, 1827.

With the Treaty of Washington, most of the Creek chiefs, including Menawa, had agreed to a final peace and never again opposed the United States. There was not a final peace for the Creeks. The Creek land rights set down in the Treaty of Washington were ultimately ineffectual. Settlers continued to ignore Creek land rights in Georgia and Alabama and, in many cases, defrauded Creeks out of their land.

Georgia and Governor Troup, William McIntosh's cousin, refused to recognize the Treaty of Washington. Troup announced that he planned to proceed with the land lottery that would distribute land gained in the Second Treaty of Indian Springs to Georgia settlers. President John Quincy Adams attempted to enforce the authority of the federal government and even threatened to intervene by bringing U.S. troops down to Georgia. Governor Troup called the president's bluff and began to raise the Georgia Militia. Adams backed down. The lottery proceeded.

Days after the executions at Lock-Chau-talo-fau, the tension and violence arrived in the Atlanta area. A confrontation erupted between the Lower Creeks and the Upper Creeks, who had migrated to the area after the Red Stick War and taken up residence around Sandtown and Standing Peachtree. The skirmish occurred at Walton Spring, near the old trail that would become Marietta Street, and was later reported in the *Atlanta Constitution* in 1869:

> *Two factions occupied enemy camps, one at Walton Spring, near what is now Spring Street and Carnegie Way, the other where the Union Station would be built. In the Summer of 1825, fueled by liquor they purchased with animal skins in Decatur, the two groups began trading insults and blows. The fighting progressed to knives, tomahawks and guns. For more than two hours, the virgin forest rang with the clangor of arms and demoniac yells of drunken and infuriated savages.*

The fight culminated in a battle in a grove of oak trees on Alabama, between Whitehall and Pryor (the Sandtown trail and the current location between Peachtree Fountains Plaza and Underground Atlanta). The carnival of death went on until every actor in the tragic scene was disemboweled, or rendered utterly helpless, while in the adjacent thicket were scattered the dead and the dying who were engaged in the fight. The whole numbering not less than fifty, which was probably the entire combative strength of the two factions.

9

THE SECOND CREEK WAR AND THE LITTLE CANNON IN DECATUR

The last chapter in the saga of the Creek Indians in Georgia before their removal directly involved several Decatur residents and the cannon that now sits on the Decatur Square. After their land in Georgia had been sold to the United States and issued out through the land lottery system, the first group of Creeks who had supported William McIntosh voluntarily left Georgia for land at Fort Gibson in Oklahoma (near present-day Muscogee, Oklahoma) in 1827. They brought 703 Creeks and 86 slaves. About a year later, 400 more left. In 1829, 1,200 more left from Fort Bainbridge and Line Creek, some by land and many by steamship up the Mississippi River.

The last of the voluntary emigrants from Georgia arrived in Oklahoma during the month of September 1829. They immediately had to face a cholera epidemic and suffer raids from western Indians like the Plains Apache, who had not at all agreed to hand over the land in the West to these new arrivals.

Many of the Creeks who had left voluntarily chose to return to land still owned by the Upper Creeks in Alabama rather than stay in Oklahoma. More groups of Creeks removed themselves from Alabama and left for Oklahoma in 1835 and 1836, but most Creeks chose to stay on the land they still owned in Alabama. Those who returned from Oklahoma probably told convincing stories about why to avoid going west.

Partial refuge in Alabama provided short-lived relief. Settlers continued to ignore Creek rights to the land and settled within their borders. The state governments continued to refuse to enforce Creek land rights. Several skirmishes broke out among the Creeks and the settlers. The tide of settlers was still rising and steadily washing over the Creeks in Alabama.

In 1836, Creeks in Alabama had had enough and took up arms against the Americans once again. They were partly inspired by the recent success of their cousins, the Seminoles, to resist the Americans. The violence began in Russell County, Alabama, with sporadic attacks on intruding settlers. The governor mustered the troops and ordered them to "be prepared to march at a moment's warning." The Calhoun brothers of Decatur both responded eagerly to the call.

Creeks from the towns of Chehaw, Yuchi and Hitchiti attacked squatters on Creek land and burned down their plantations in present-day Alabama. The conflict then attracted the attention of the federal government. Andrew Jackson traveled south to quash the disruptions in what has come to be called the Second Creek War of 1836.

When the conflict crossed the border of Alabama and entered Georgia, a call to arms went out from the Georgia governor on May 15, 1836. A force of Creek warriors invaded the little town of Roanoke, Georgia, along the Chattahoochee River about thirty miles south of Columbus. (The town of Roanoke is now beneath Walter F. George Reservoir.) The Creeks burned the town to the ground and killed twelve of its residents. The surviving townspeople fled into the woods.

The governor thought more forces were needed from Georgia. In June 1836, the governor required "the voluntary enlistment or draft of every sixth man from the 54th Regiment of the Georgia Militia to form the DeKalb Independent Guards" to bolster the size of the Georgia forces. William Ezzard was elected to become their captain.

Ezekiel Calhoun's infantry left Decatur in July 1836 with eighty-four men. On the infantry's departure, the ladies of Decatur presented the company with an American flag to carry into battle. The DeKalb companies were all sent to the southwestern part of the state near Columbus, where fighting was already in progress. After arriving, they were stationed at Fort Macreary in Columbus. The cannon was taken to West Point, Georgia, by E.N. Calhoun's company.

On July 31, 1836, James Calhoun was in command (as a temporary position) of the DeKalb Cavalry when they attacked a band of around thirty Indians who were hiding in a swamp on the plantation of a Mr. Quall near Columbus, Georgia. An account of the engagement appeared in the *Columbus Enquirer* after the battle:

THE WAR NOT YET ENDED

On Sunday morning last a severe engagement took place as usual, between the Georgians and the Indians, in the neighborhood of Mr. Quall's [Quarles in another article] *plantation, above Roanoke. We have not received the particulars of the fight but learned that information was given to the forces stationed at Fort McCrary, that fresh signs of the Indians had been discovered in a swamp in Mr. Quall's plantation; upon which Captain Calhoun, of DeKalb County, with a command of ninety men, were dispatched in pursuit of the enemy. In scouring the place, a fresh trail was found, leading out of the swamp in the direction of Lumpkin. It was followed. In a short time, the party came up with a small gang of Indians, of thirty or more and commenced the fight. The Indians soon fled, leaving seven of their number killed. The whites, after the first skirmish, supposed the Indians whipped and the fight over; but they found that this advance party was a mere decoy, to draw them into the midst of their enemies, by whom they soon found themselves completely flanked on both sides. The battle was renewed, but the ammunition of the whites being exhausted, they were compelled to retreat. In the engagement, the whites lost five soldiers killed and several wounded. Among the slain were, Mr. Colly, (overseer for D.P. Hillhouse, Esq.,) a brave man and much respected; a Mr. Willis and Dr. Orr, of DeKalb—the names of the others are not yet known to us. It is said that the whites had only three rounds of cartridges apiece when the fight first commenced—a very unfortunate oversight, indeed, and if true, wholly unpardonable in the commanding officer. Something of this sort was surely the matter or the DeKalb boys would never have turned their backs upon their enemy, although they may have outnumbered them three to one.*

The two other men lost were John Willis, son of James Willis of Snapfinger, and Matthew J. Orr, son of Robert Orr of Sandtown. Robert Billups was also killed in a separate battle during the war.

Following the War of 1836, any sentiment toward assimilation of the Creeks was gone. All Creeks were set on the path to be forcibly removed from both Georgia and Alabama. Most were put on steamboats out of Mobile and New Orleans and then marched to Fort Gibson in Oklahoma. Remaining "friendly" Creeks were rounded up and sent along behind them in August and September 1836. The governor of Georgia after George Gilmer, Wilson Lumpkin left office in 1835 but presided over the removal of the Cherokees from Georgia at the request of President Andrew Jackson.

The Decatur cavalry in the Creek conflict of 1836. *Illustrations by Chulsan Um.*

The forced removals continued all the way into 1837 and 1838. Voluntary removals from Alabama continued through the 1840s and 1850s, and some Creeks still remained behind. A small number of them were able to stay in their homeland and avoid the U.S. government. They formed the Poarch Band of Creeks that still resides in southern Alabama. In all, the

Creek removals from the Southeast to Oklahoma accounted for around twenty-three thousand Creek people.

Menawa, the Upper Creek chief who had led much of the Red Stick War and the Battle of Horseshoe Bend, participated in the Creek War of 1836 alongside the Americans. He felt it was his duty to be true to the promises he had made in the Treaty of Washington.

The chief they called Great Warrior was old now, and his body had been wounded many times. He had only one wish for which he strenuously argued with the Americans. This was that he be allowed to remain in his homeland and abide by the laws of the United States. He wanted to assimilate. At first, he was granted this consideration for the help he had given them. The permission was later rescinded, and Menawa was ordered to leave with all the others.

Portrait of Menawa, "The Great Warrior," later in his life. *Library of Congress.*

After Menawa was informed that he would have to leave, he grew quiet and morose. He avoided questions about when he would go and seemed to avoid establishing a final day of departure. It was suggested to him at one point that part of his reluctance may have been out of fear of meeting up with the followers of McIntosh who were already waiting there in Oklahoma.

In reply, he said, "They do not know me who suppose I can be influenced by fear. I desire peace but would not turn my back on danger. I know there will be bloodshed, but I am not afraid. I have been a man of blood all my life. Now I am old and wish for peace."

Before he took his final leave, he spent a last night in Oakfuskee where he had grown up and become chief (now beneath the southern part of Lake Martin in Alabama). He stayed there one night and began the journey to Oklahoma on foot the next morning. After crossing the Tallapoosa River where the greatest battle of his life had been fought and lost, he seemed as if he had forgotten something. He was asked by one of his companions if he'd like to return to Oakfuskee. In response, he said, "No! Last evening, I saw the sunset for the last time, and its light shines upon the treetops and the land and the water, that I am never to look upon again. No other evening will come, bringing to Menawa's eyes the rays of the setting sun upon the home he has left forever!"

Menawa continued west. From there, his story passed into history and American legend. His name is not listed as having arrived in Oklahoma, nor was there any report of his death. No one knows if Menawa reached Oklahoma or stopped along the way to live in hiding or died somewhere along his journey and was buried in a secret spot between Georgia and Oklahoma.

10

GEORGIA'S SLUGGISH COMMITMENT TO THE VISION OF SOUTHERN RAILROADS

Y ears after the land officially became part of Georgia in 1821, Atlanta was founded as a direct result of the country's westward expansion to the Mississippi River and a reaction to the recent wildly rapid growth of the city of New Orleans. Most of the history of the American South before 1835 was led by Savannah and Charleston. These were the region's social, political, cultural and economic centers. After the country expanded west to the Mississippi River, this quickly changed. Tariffs had caused serious declines in the business for imports to the United States. Years of farming had exhausted much of the cleared land in North Carolina, South Carolina and Georgia. Charleston and Savannah fell from glory. The commerce coming from the new western United States (Missouri, Arkansas, Illinois and the vast Iowa territory) far outstripped the South and the rest of the country.

There were no roads into or out of these new territories. The primary way all this cargo got to market from the west was by river. Everything was floated down the Ohio, Missouri or Arkansas Rivers, and all of it eventually arrived on the Mississippi River. The vast majority of all U.S. trade was coming through on these routes.

In the 1840s, there was a fleet of 450 steamboats and 4,000 flatboats operating on Mark Twain's Mississippi River. If they were full, with a cargo of lead from Wisconsin, corn from Iowa, cotton from Arkansas or tobacco from Missouri, they were headed for New Orleans. New Orleans received and shipped twice as much of the produce coming from the West as all other American ports combined. It was the second-largest port in the country and, at one point, the third-largest city in the country with a population that doubled every fifteen years or so.

With the growth of new transportation technology, opportunities were emerging for other cities to divert trade that had been going to New Orleans. The voyage down the Mississippi was slow, hot and humid. New Orleans had few warehouses to protect perishable goods. Shipments sat on the dock and baked in the sun. Pork and beef spoiled. Tobacco wilted. Grain swelled and softened. A faster, shorter route that ran more east–west instead of north–south would improve commerce from the West and reap the rewards. A system of railroads could move goods out of the West faster and cheaper than steamboats and bring traffic back to the rest of the South.

Georgia was early in proposing to become a core link in the southern railroad network but late in beginning its construction. As early as 1826, the state commissioned two important surveying projects to investigate the potential of connecting the Tennessee River with the Atlantic Ocean and connecting the Savannah River with the Flint River. The survey between Tennessee and the Atlantic was particularly interesting because it involved venturing into what was then still Cherokee territory. The two people chosen for the task were Hamilton Fulton, as chief engineer, and Wilson Lumpkin, a former state representative and then a governor, to represent the state's interests. Fulton was a middle-aged Scotsman who had recently emigrated from England. Lumpkin would become a principal player in the construction of the Georgia railroads and the founding of Atlanta.

The survey showed that the Georgia land was well suited to a railroad. Had the survey gotten more attention in 1826 and the legislature moved with greater confidence in the future of railroads in the South, the fortunes and fates of Atlanta and the South could have been much different in the 1840s. Unfortunately, the idea of a trans-Georgia railroad was ahead of its time. The Georgia Board of Public Works that sponsored the survey was disbanded before the end of the year.

It took until 1833 for Georgia to finally feel the spur to begin railroad projects. The citizens of Savannah were at last realizing they had fallen behind their friendly rivals in Charleston. As the *Macon Telegraph* phrased it, "Old Yamacraw was waking up." In October 1833, they petitioned the city to support a railroad, and the city appropriated $500,000 to the project. The Central Railroad and Banking Company of Georgia was chartered on December 20, 1833, to construct a line from Savannah to Macon with

Wilson Lumpkin, former governor of Georgia, who had much to do with the founding of Atlanta. *Library of Congress*.

several planned branches. At last, there would be rails slowly beginning to extend from Georgia's coast toward the interior.

The very next day, the people of Augusta ensured their place in the network by chartering the Georgia Railroad on December 21, 1833. The Georgia Railroad would construct a line from Augusta to Athens with branches to Forsyth.

Just two days later, the Monroe Railroad (later the Macon and Western Railroad) was chartered on December 23, 1833. It would connect with the Central Railroad from Savannah and through Macon and on to Forsyth, presumably on its way farther north to connect with other railroads yet to be designed. The South Carolina Railroad would come close to connecting with the Georgia Railroad by reaching Hamburg, across the river from Augusta, but goods would need to be unloaded in Augusta and ferried across to Hamburg.

The central arteries from Savannah and Augusta across Georgia were now in motion, but they needed to connect into the west to be effective. They needed to meet other railroads outside the state to connect into the western river valleys. Pressure was now high for the state to contribute its part of the plan.

When the state legislature met in 1834, the construction of the state railroad became the immediate focus of that year's session. The State of Georgia finally formed a resolve on December 20, 1834. "Resolved, that the times require, and the resources of the State authorize, a scheme of internal improvement from the Seaboard of this State to the interior by a railroad on the faith and credit of the State as a great State Work." Partners were still needed to form connections to the Mississippi River.

As he prepared to leave office in 1834, Governor Lumpkin would still be performing an important task for the construction of the railroads. The 1826 survey showed that the best route out of the state was northwest through Cherokee territory. The state had to remove the Creeks and the Cherokees from the state in order to lay the tracks through their territory. Much of northern Georgia was already populated by American settlers after the discovery of gold in the region in 1829. They pushed the passage of the Indian Removal Act signed by Andrew Jackson in 1830. This authorized the president to grant land to the Indians west of the Mississippi in exchange for land within state borders.

The last piece of land was gained from the Cherokees on December 29, 1835, through the Treaty of New Echota signed a month after Lumpkin left office. After serving as governor, Lumpkin was now requested to reenter political life by President Andrew Jackson, and from 1834 to 1836, he acted on the president's behalf to execute the treaties for the removal of the Cherokees from the American South and clear the way for the state railroad. This overall action is most well known as the Trail of Tears. Despite the key role he played in the promotion of the State Railroad in Georgia, Lumpkin felt the greatest accomplishment of his tenure was the role he played in removing the Cherokees from Georgia.

As he prepared to leave office, Lumpkin had grown concerned about the plans being made in other states to reach to the Ohio River Valley with railroads. Plans were progressing with little input from the State of Georgia. The Georgia legislature finally responded and agreed in 1835 to conduct new surveys with the objective of showing the superiority of a connection to the Cincinnati and Charleston Railroad line in Georgia. Governor Schley, who succeeded Lumpkin, hired Abbott Hall Brisbane for the job. Brisbane is another of the handful of people who unknowingly made several important decisions that determined central elements in the creation of Atlanta. He had previously earned renown for his participation in the Seminole Wars commanding the South Carolina Volunteers. This earned him the nickname "South Carolina Hotspur."

In cities around Georgia, state legislators and railroad supporters went into action in 1836, holding meetings and lavish dinners to lobby for railroad funding and persuade other railroad officials to cooperate with Georgia. At the Tennessee State Convention in Knoxville in July, it was revealed that charters for new railroads had already been granted to support the grand plan for the Cincinnati and Charleston Railroad in the states of Tennessee, South Carolina, North Carolina and Kentucky and that none of them included plans to connect with Georgia. Tennessee's charter was the only one that included any mention of Georgia as a branch line that might connect to Knoxville. Georgia's lethargic start in the railroad race had left it far behind the rest of the South.

In light of the knowledge gained from the Knoxville Convention, a Georgia convention was called to be held in Macon to expedite the proposal for a state-owned railroad in Georgia and catch up to the progress being made in other parts of the South. Along with the delegates from across Georgia, two railroad companies attended the convention in Macon: the Georgia Railroad Company and the Monroe Railroad Company. The resolutions passed at the Macon Convention were that (1) The state must build a central railroad as a state project, (2) private companies should be encouraged to build branch roads from any points on the trunk line and (3) special attention was directed to branch lines to Athens, Forsyth and Columbus. (Athens and Forsyth were the northern terminal points of the Georgia and Monroe Railroads.)

Surprisingly, the report of the Macon convention also included a statement of intention to pursue a new course other than its connection with the Cincinnati and Charleston. The proposed state-funded railroad would connect north out of Georgia to Chattanooga.

> *It is a matter about which no doubt is entertained by those well acquainted with the localities of the country, that an excellent route for the road, requiring not a single inclined plane or a stationary engine, can be obtained from Ross' Landing* [Chattanooga] *to some point on the Chattahoochee in DeKalb County.*
> —*report of the Macon Railroad Convention, 1836*

This route took the plans farther to the west rather than connect toward Columbia, South Carolina. The delegates believed they had a more eager partner with Tennessee than with a connection into South Carolina, and this model would be superior in bringing goods to Savannah instead of Charleston and make Georgia more central to the overall network.

Governor Schley did his part by pushing for support in the Georgia legislature using the survey conducted by Abbott Hall Brisbane. In the 1836 session, William Washington Gordon, a member of the House and the president of the Central Railroad Company, introduced a bill for the chartering of a new railroad at the state's expense.

The bill to fund a major railroad at the expense of the State of Georgia passed by a vote of 76–65 on December 21, 1836. After some debate, the bill carried out the resolutions from the convention in Macon. The state railroad would be built toward Ross' Landing (Chattanooga) rather than join it with the Cincinnati and Charleston Railroad.

Specifically, the bill contained some famous phrases in Atlanta history because they are the first specific references to where the city would be founded. It said the railroad would be built:

> *from some point on the Tennessee line near the Tennessee River, commencing at or near Rossville in the most direct practicable route to some point on the southeastern bank of the Chattahoochee River and which shall be most eligible for the extension of branch railroads thence to Athens, Madison, Milledgeville, Forsyth, and Columbus, and to any other points which may be designated by the engineer or engineers surveying the same as the most proper and practicable, and on which the Legislature may hereafter determine…. said railroad shall cross the Chattahoochee River at some point between Campbellton in Campbell County and Wynn's Ferry in Hall County…. said railroad shall be known and distinguished as the Western & Atlantic Railroad of the state of Georgia. [emphasis added]*

On December 10, 1836, the charter of the Monroe Railroad had already been amended, and in Section XVIII it is stated:

> *The said Monroe Railroad and Banking Company, shall be, and are hereby authorized to extend their aforesaid railroad continuously from and beyond Forsyth, in a northward direction, to such point near, or on, the Chattahoochee River, and shall hereinafter be determined on, as the southern termination of any railroad to be constructed by, or under the authority of this State,—from the Tennessee line, through the counties of the late Cherokee country, to or near the Chattahoochee,—below the mountains,—*

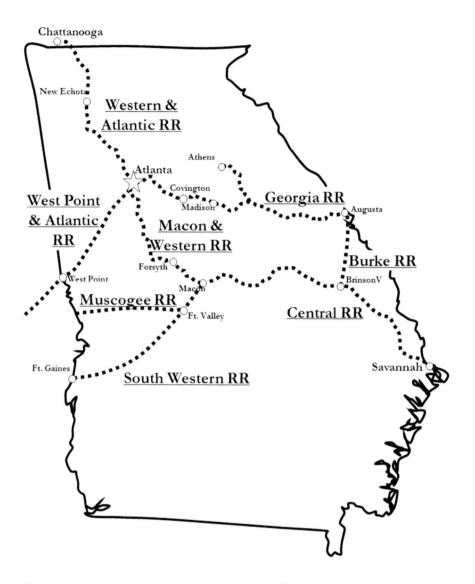

Georgia railroads in 1851, showing how the three main lines met in Atlanta. *Sketch by the author using sources from Library of Congress.*

and shall be compelled and obliged to join their said railroad to any railroad that may be so hereafter built as aforesaid, so as to admit the continuous travel of cars and vehicles, from the one to the other road.

On December 21, 1836, the Georgia Railroad and Banking Company (a previous amendment in 1836 changed the name from the Georgia Railroad) charter was amended "to continue and extend their railroad from the town of Madison, in Morgan county to pass through or near the town of Covington, in Newton County, and to connect with the railroad authorized to be constructed from the Tennessee line, near the Tennessee river, to the southeastern bank of the Chattachoochee River."

As a result of these charters, without anyone knowing it, they had finally agreed to locate and fund the location of the new city of Atlanta.

II

Staking Out the Western and Atlantic

The original plan was for the railroad toward the Mississippi to terminate in Chattanooga. Goods from the West would first be brought to Tuscumbia, Alabama, down the Tennessee River by boat. They then could be brought past the shoals in the Tennessee River with a forty-four-mile railroad trip to Decatur, Alabama. Then, they would be loaded back on boats to be brought to Chattanooga to connect with the Western and Atlantic.

Boat transportation on the Tennessee was too expensive and slow. It quickly became evident that this complicated route would be inadequate to reestablish southern transportation commerce. To make the southern vision of diverting trade from New Orleans a reality, the railroad would need to reach the Mississippi. The route would reach all the way from the coast to Memphis through the junction in the middle of the state (the junction that would become Atlanta). There would also be a line through the junction or through Macon and passing through West Point to Vicksburg, Mississippi.

Governor Schley interviewed several engineers for the position to survey the route for the Western and Atlantic Railroad. The person he eventually settled on could not have been more well equipped for the task. Stephen Harriman Long was a distinguished engineer in the Army Corps of Engineers and professor of mathematics at West Point. Long had literally written the book on the engineering of railroad construction. He had previously conducted the survey for the Baltimore and Ohio Railroad, and during that time, he wrote the first manual on the building of railroads ever published in the United States. The army agreed to allow Long to contract out a third of his time to the State of Georgia.

Once hired, Long set out for the area around the Chattahoochee on May 13, 1837. Assisting him in the survey work were three engineers: William S. Whitwell, Thomas Stockton and Abbott Hall Brisbane, the engineer who conducted the original survey to locate a railroad in Georgia with Wilson Lumpkin over ten years earlier. Brisbane was finally getting a chance to make his recommendations a reality.

The most specific stipulation was that the railroad needed to cross the Chattahoochee somewhere between Winn's Ferry and Campbellton and reach a point that would make it as convenient as possible to meet other railroads coming from Augusta, Macon and Columbus. Several points on the Chattahoochee were evaluated for the crossing, including at Sandtown and Sweet Water Creek. Two routes were selected for final consideration. The first was near Pittman's Ferry at the present location of Medlock Bridge. The second was near Montgomery's Ferry just south of the Peachtree Creek, Standing Peachtree and Fort Peachtree.

Long and his assistants met at the Chattahoochee on July 4, 1837, to select a final location for the crossing. Before the end of that day, Long found a potential crossing point and planted a stake two miles below Pittman's Ferry at the present location of the Medlock Bridge. They then tried to find a route up to the Etowah that fit within the limits for Long's specifications regarding grade and turns. They couldn't find a route though. The Pittman's Ferry crossing point was abandoned.

The engineers then visited Standing Peachtree to examine the second candidate for the crossing closer to Montgomery's Ferry. Preliminary readings north and south of the ferry had already indicated this might be a more feasible route if they could just find the crossing. They found a likely spot 1,500 feet below Montgomery's Ferry where there is a high bluff on the eastern bank. This is now just south of Atlanta Road and the Atlanta River Intake facility. Later in 1850, the bridge built at the location chosen by Long, Brisbane and Stockton was abandoned for one eight hundred feet farther downriver that required less of a turn and grade on the southeast bank.

Long then returned to Milledgeville with the governor and then went back to New York to attend to personal business. It fell to his assistants, Brisbane and Stockton, to survey the land between the Chattahoochee and the headwaters of the South River for a route inland from the crossing. On some date close to September 10, 1837, Abbott Hall Brisbane pulled a stake out of his bags and hammered it into the ground close to the intersection of

Driving of the stake by Stephen Long at the proposed terminus of the Western and Atlantic Railroad. *Atlanta History Center*.

several old trails running through the Georgia woods. He had selected and marked the spot that would become downtown Atlanta. However, the spot he chose was not destined to be the city center for perplexing reasons that would occur later.

On September 10, 1837, Long wrote to the governor:

> *The result of the levels to the ridge near Decatur, DeKalb County, which you authorized me to run proved altogether flattering; the ascent to the main ridge, <u>where we left a bench mark</u>, is only two hundred eighty-five feet above the level of the Chattahoochee, which is to be reached with a distance of eight miles—which at our assumed grades is attainable with ease. In fine [sic], sir, nothing more is now required than to realize by physical ability that which intellectual enterprise has so handsomely planned. This I leave in your hands.* [emphasis added]

12

John Thrasher and the Founding of Terminus

John Thrasher was a young man of only twenty when he rode the forty or so miles over from his parents' home in Newton County to the spot in the woods that the engineers of the Monroe Railroad Company had pointed out to him. He probably rode past the correct spot first in order to stop in at the Whitehall Inn for a meal. As a stagecoach stop, it was the best-known landmark outside of Decatur and a good place to take some time and ask for more directions. From there, he would have wound back up the Sandtown trail that led to an old Creek town by that name until it met with the Peachtree trail that led to the old Creek and Cherokee town of Standing Peachtree. At this intersection, he turned left and walked his horse a quarter of a mile or so up the trail that led to Marietta and stopped there. This was the spot where the Monroe Railroad planned to meet up with the Georgia Railroad coming from the east and the Western and Atlantic that would run north to Chattanooga. There was a problem in making that meeting though. The ground at this point was too low for the Monroe to meet smoothly with the Western and Atlantic. An embankment would need to be built to raise up the ground and make a smooth junction with the other railroads.

The Monroe called for bids to do the job, and Thrasher won the contract at a price of $25,000. The embankment John Thrasher and his laborers would build, called the Monroe Embankment, remains today near the Georgia World Congress Center as the oldest structure within the city limits original to this pioneering period.

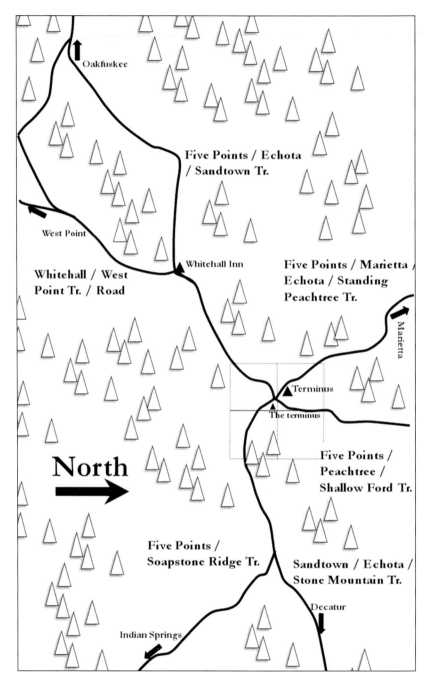

Major trails as they would have existed in 1839 when John Thrasher arrived in the area.
Sketch by the author using sources of the DeKalb History Center and the Atlanta History Center.

The countryside Thrasher found was lovely, thick forest of oak and Georgia pine. The shrubbery consisted largely of sourwood, gooseberry and Allegheny chinquapin. There were several beautiful springs nearby that rilled their way down to the Chattahoochee and the south fork of the Ocmulgee.

It was not yet known as Terminus or Marthasville and certainly not as Atlanta. For unknown reasons, some of the people who lived in the area called it Black Ankle. It was also simply called Cane-Brake by some. Since Charner Humphries had erected the Whitehall Inn in 1837, the southern part of the area was known by that name. South of there was generally called Black Hall. John Thrasher gave a description of how he found the place:

> *When I arrived in this place in 1839, the country was entirely covered by forest. There was but one house here at the time and that stood where the old post office was formerly located; it was built of logs and was occupied by an old woman and her daughter about sixteen years of age. I found a man named Thurman living in the country nearby.*

Though Thrasher didn't come across all of them at the time, there were others living in the dense woods since the Creeks had gone west. One of the first to arrive before Thrasher was John Young. He was a rancher running his cattle in the area. He built a small house for himself and a small log cabin to house an Indian family he had hired to watch over his herd. This was probably the cabin Thrasher found occupied by an old woman and her daughter. Hardy Ivy also made his way to the area in 1833. He owned two hundred acres along what is now Peachtree Street to Cain Street and back toward Ponce de Leon Avenue.

Thrasher's first task was to set up facilities for the workers who would soon be joining him. He and his partner, Lochlin Johnson, set up a camp store, the first store in the Atlanta area, which they dubbed Johnson and Thrasher. After that, he started constructing simple shanties to house the workers who would arrive soon.

Thrasher sent for and gradually assembled a good crew to work on the embankment. As the work progressed, Thrasher needed more right of way to build the embankment. He petitioned the DeKalb Superior Court to establish a committee to assess damages that would be caused by the construction and paid for by the Monroe Railroad Company.

The little town they created together was called the terminus or simply Terminus for short. It has often been called Thrasherville. There is a historical marker in downtown Atlanta commemorating Thrasher's community by

Johnson & Thrasher's Camp Store in 1839. *Atlanta History Center*.

that name. There was never a place called Thrasherville, though, not even by John Thrasher himself. He had another idea in mind for the town he wanted to create. Not far from Terminus, Thrasher found another partner, Lemuel Dean, and they purchased land where they thought the Western and Atlantic Railroad would meet the Monroe Railroad and planned to call their future town by the melodious name of Deantown. Unfortunately, the Deantown plan never really got off the ground, and the common reference to the area stayed Terminus.

Life was happy in Terminus. Descriptions of it often include mention of parties and games as central elements. Throughout his life, John Thrasher was unanimously described as an affable man. He was well known for generosity in Newton County and in the areas surrounding his new home in Terminus. He was called "Cousin John" by most who knew him. This was partly because he had such a wide family around the area where he grew up. Many people in Newton County were indeed his cousins, so he developed a habit of only half-jokingly calling most people "cousin." People also called him Cousin John simply out of affection.

There must have been a strong spirit of opportunity and thanksgiving in Terminus. The residents of Thrasher's little community lived in little shanties with dirt floors, but this was a significant improvement in their standard of living. Nearly all of Cousin John's thirty or so workers had come from Europe, where jobs were very scarce. Most were from Ireland, where the horror of the Great Famine was just beginning.

Millions of Irish, English, Germans and Scots made their way through the ports of New York, Savannah and Charleston during these years, and many of them found their way to Terminus for work in some way connected to the railroads. From the 1820s to the 1840s, around 90 percent of immigrants to the United States came from Ireland, England and Germany. Among these groups, the Irish were by far the largest. In the 1820s, nearly 60,000 Irish immigrated to the United States. In the 1830s, the number grew to 235,000, and in the 1840s, the number skyrocketed to 845,000.

Here in the warm forest with steady work, money and food coming, it must have been a relief to many of them. Thrasher got more than he had bargained for in a delightful way when his work progressed to the point he needed to hire a foreman:

> *I was building the Monroe Embankment. My foreman was a man named Mulligan. You might suspect from his name that he was Irish. He was a good workman. I got him from the State road because he had experience in*

railroad work, and I needed such a man to look after my laborers. Mulligan was a married man, and so were others of my laborers—the most of whom lived in the neighborhood of the present Presbyterian Church (present site of the Federal Reserve Bank). These shacks were rude cabins made of roughly sawed timber. All of them had dirt floors. There was not a plank floor among them all.

Mrs. Mulligan heard that the shacks were not floored with boards and she refused to move down here with her husband unless her cabin was floored with planks. She was the foreman's wife, and she felt that she was entitled to something better than a dirt floor. Mulligan would not stay with me unless his wife moved down, and so there was nothing for me to do but to buy the lumber and put a wooden floor in the Mulligan shack; and so, I had to go out to Collier's Mill for the material. Well, I bought a load or two of puncheon and laid the best floor I could for Mrs. Mulligan. Her husband though it would please her, and she came down.

No sooner was she fairly installed in her new home than she announced that she would give a ball and the wives of all the other men who were working on the railroad were invited, and so were every other man's wife.

The first society of Atlanta was there, and it was swell affair, or we thought it was. Mrs. Mulligan was mistress of ceremonies, and she said that I would have to dance the first set with her. I had on a pair of rough high-topped boots, but that gave Mrs. Mulligan no concern. She said that it did not matter at all, at all. We circled around a few times, and the heel of one of my boots got caught in the floor, and the heel came off. I finished the dance in a hippity-hop sort of fashion, but, as they say nowadays, everything went then. It was a crème de la crème affair, and the function established Mrs. Mulligan as the leader of the four hundred. She was quite a fine-looking woman of strong physique, and if anybody had questioned her leadership she could have established her claim to the championship as well as to the leadership.

But you know how women are about things. If one has something her neighbor wants it too. Well, sir, the day after the ball a delegation of the men came to me and announced that their wives wanted plank floors in their shacks, and they declared that if I didn't put them in the houses every blessed man of them would quit work.

I had to send out to Collier's Mill and get a good many loads of puncheons to floor the other shacks. That is the history of the first social function that ever occurred in Atlanta (then Terminus) after the Indians left this county.

The smart set has changed a good deal in the years which had elapsed since Mrs. Mulligan's ball, but 1 bet that they never enjoyed a dance more than the first one was enjoyed.
—John Thrasher

13

The Hard Times Arrive and the Railroads Apply the Brakes

As Cousin John wheeled the lovely Mrs. Mulligan about the first wooden floor in what would be Atlanta, few if any of the other party guests and coworkers realized how short-lived the prosperity and harmony of Terminus would be.

When Terminus was founded and Thrasher made plans for the metropolis of Deantown, the United States was hanging its hopes for future prosperity on the opening of the West and the growth of transportation across the country. Major construction projects had created steady jobs and growth in the South as they had for Cousin John and the other residents of Terminus. Cotton prices rose. The South prospered.

The country's leaders weren't the only ones depending on new territories and railroads for growth. Every American citizen looked toward the wave of improvements as a way to make their fortune. There was vast speculation on real estate. People were purchasing any patch of land where there was a slim chance the railroad might make a stop. Most of these purchases were being made on credit, and most of them were bought for prices that turned out to be well above their real, eventual market value. A massive real estate bubble developed.

This bubble kept inflating through the 1830s as the railroads spread to new towns and everyone tried to guess where they would stop next. The pop was inevitable. Its exact timing was hastened, and its severity was heightened by a batch of three colossally misconceived pieces of legislation promoted by President Andrew Jackson that dismantled the federal banking system.

Jackson had a well-established distaste for the federal government and particularly for the banks.

Jackson and his administration didn't realize the important role the federal banks played until it was too late. The dismantling of the federal banking system removed control over credit rates for capital. As money moved out of northern banks to the South and the West, large banks and financial institutions in the Northeast started making fewer loans. The Specie Circular of 1836 that required all real estate transaction of federal land to be conducted in hard currency gave the slowdown a final tip, bringing everything to a halt.

The bubble burst in the spring of 1837. The wild real estate speculation in the South and the West collided with the effects of this legislation with a spectacular crash. As people tried to withdraw their money, overextended banks closed their doors and many collapsed entirely. Much of the capital used to fund the railroads up to this point, including the funding of the Monroe Railroad in particular, came from northern banks and investors. This crisis developed into a depression that lasted into the early 1840s. These were the "Hard Times."

As Jonathan Norcross, Atlanta's fourth mayor, put it:

> *Instead of recession merely, it was a crash as it has ever since been called— an explosion, that was heard and felt throughout the civilized world; an explosion, the effects of which are almost beyond the power of words to describe or the mind of man to measure, an explosion, a crash and paralysis in industrial and business circles from this this country did not fully recover in ten years…detrimental alike to the industry, the resources and the morals of the people.*

The plan for Georgia's railroad network teetered very close to complete failure but continued slowly forward. By 1843, the Western and Atlantic was still unfinished above Marietta and progress seemed to be slowing with every additional day. The taxes bore heavily upon the suffering public of Georgia, and the Hard Times had made funding through loans difficult. The Georgia legislature considered selling off its partially built railroad or perhaps even abandoning it. This proposal was narrowly defeated by just one vote.

The Monroe Railroad, the only privately funded road planned to reach Terminus, soldiered on but slowed its progress in 1843 and was forced to declare bankruptcy in 1844. It was then purchased and became the Macon and Western Railroad in 1845.

Though progress dropped to a snail's pace, the risk of abandoning the projects was too great. Georgia continued most of its grand visions to join the great southern web of iron. Though most projects were not canceled outright, their costs were cut drastically. Southern projects were able to reduce costs in a way northern and western railroads could not. Southern construction shifted toward greater use of slave labor. By the fall of 1839, contractors on the Georgia Railroad were exclusively using enslaved laborers. Convicts were also put to work building the state's railroads beginning in 1843. This labor shift played out in Terminus in 1840 or 1841. John Thrasher saw the change firsthand:

> *I was working about twenty-five white men and perhaps as many young negroes. The negroes drove the carts. The white men I paid $16 a month, and they boarded themselves. It was hard work, I confess. One morning I blew the horn, they came marching up and walked right by me, calling out that they would not go to work unless they got more wages. I let them go, but I was in trouble. The negroes could not do much but drive the mules. I sat down in front of the store, and smoked and thought, for I was in trouble sure enough. While I was sitting there a preacher rode up and asked me if Mr. Thrasher lived there. I told him that Mr. Thrasher lived about thirty-five miles from there. He insisted that he had been told that John Thrasher lived at Terminus. "Oh, if you want to see John Thrasher, that is me." I replied.*
>
> *That preacher wanted to know if I would hire 25 negro men. That was exactly what I wanted, and I struck a trade with him just as soon as he got down off his horse, and I told my cook to get up the best dinner she could. I gave him $16 a month for his negroes, and boarded them, and he brought them in to me that night. That was the beginning and end of the first labor strike that ever was known here.*

The equation Thrasher gives us was simple and illustrates why railroad labor in the South quickly shifted to the use of slaves. Much of the work to build the southern railroads was done without even using cash. Planters who owned property near the lines, partly encouraged by the falling prices for cotton due to the financial crisis, hired out their slaves to grade the land and lay the tracks at low costs or in exchange for shares in the company in lieu of cash.

It was well known for a long time that the railroad companies themselves also bought slaves to work on the railroads, but the apology for this despicable practice was late in coming. The Georgia Railroad and Banking Company later became Wachovia Bank, now Wells Fargo. In 2005, G. Kennedy Thompson, the chairman and CEO of Wachovia Bank, issued a public apology on behalf of the company for having used more than five hundred slaves in the construction of the Georgia Railroad.

What then happened to Mrs. Mulligan and her husband and his coworkers once the Irish laborers were let go? In the case of the Mulligans, their whereabouts through the 1840s are unknown. We know what became of many of their fellow immigrants.

In 1841, two of the Irish who had arrived to work on the railroad, Patrick Porter and Patrick Jordan, became naturalized citizens of the United States and settled in other parts of DeKalb County. In September 1844, several more Irish were naturalized in Dekalb County. Many more stayed and became successful farmers, craftsmen and merchants. Today, in Georgia, the highest numbers of people with Irish ancestry still live in counties closest to Atlanta: Fulton, Gwinnett, DeKalb and Cherokee.

Most of the laborers who came to work on the railroad in and around Terminus were not so lucky to have both the skills and the means to take up farming or some other legitimate trade. They either moved on, probably west following the railroads, or stuck it out in the best ways they could.

14

THE MYSTERY OF THE MOVING TERMINUS

The Zero Mile Post planted by the Western and Atlantic Railroad is a well-known item of interest in Atlanta. It is now housed in the Atlanta History Center. For many years, it was located under the Central Avenue viaduct between Alabama and Wall Streets. It is generally recognized as a relic that marked the spot where engineers stood in the thick forest and dropped the post that founded Atlanta.

The pinpointing of mile zero, the terminus, conjures romantic images of Abbott Hall Brisbane dramatically drawing the stake from his bag and plunging it into the ground and defining what would become Atlanta. Unfortunately, the significance most people attach to the spot long commemorated by the Zero Mile Post is false. Or, at most, it's only partially true.

That's because a very strange thing happened in 1842 that had extremely far-reaching effects on the creation of Atlanta and continues to perplex any who are interested in Atlanta history. The location of the terminus of the State Road, the Western and Atlantic, moved about a quarter of a mile to the southeast. This is not a great distance, but in effect it might as well have been moved to another state. All previous plans for a depot and a city center and all the speculations made by people who wanted to sell the land for homes and businesses near those landmarks were now scrapped.

This was not a good time for disruptions in the plans to complete the railroad. The little progress the state had shown and the ballooning project costs were creating a growing number of detractors to continuing the project. An article in the *News and Gazette* made the feelings of some quite clear with the comments it made regarding the report of the chief engineer of the Western and Atlantic Railroad for the fourth quarter of 1842:

> *We hope the Legislature will not appropriate a dollar to the Road—but will either make arrangements to have it sold or give it away to anybody fool enough to take it. The stoppage or destruction of the "Grand Snout" and of several other Rail Roads in Georgia could not be regarded as a calamity by the people, to a majority of whom they are of no manner of benefit—but on the contrary, an injury.*

As part of measures taken to get the construction of the State Road "back on track," Governor McDonald appointed two executives. In order to get the work progressing more efficiently, he appointed Charles Garnett as the new chief engineer in place of James S. Williams. Williams had replaced William Harriman Long at the end of Long's contract but didn't stay in the job very long. To more closely manage the project's finances, he appointed Wilson Lumpkin, the former governor, as disbursing agent.

In 1826, Lumpkin had participated with Hamilton Fulton to survey Georgia and recommend its likelihood for a railroad. Disbursing agent is not a common job title today. Normally, it is a person who is responsible for determining the correct amount of money to pay out to investors in dividends or interest. In any definition, the primary function of the person's job is to pay out money. In Lumpkin's case, it was to more strictly manage the state funds for the building of the railroad and, given the slow pace of construction and complaints in the state legislature about the cost, to push the efficiency of the project. This is in sharp contrast to what Lumpkin actually did as disbursing agent. Lumpkin and Chief Engineer Garnett immediately focused their energies on selecting a location for the terminus even though that spot had already been selected several years prior.

Soon after Lumpkin and Garnett took their new positions, rumors began to circulate that the location of the terminus was being moved. Off and on, beginning in 1838, the idea of changing this location had been discussed but never developed into a serious movement. The news that it would change was like a bomb going off for hundreds of people associated with the building of the railroads, especially ones associated with the Georgia Railroad and the Monroe Railroad who were building to meet up with the Western and Atlantic based on the previously selected location.

The location Lumpkin and Garnett selected moved the railroad 1,200 feet to the southeast. The change required a recasting for careful plans that had already been put into motion. The Monroe Railroad had already built its embankment to fit the original plan. John Thrasher had bought up one hundred acres of land around where he expected the depot—his vision for the town of Deanville. Most important, and somewhat suspicious, this moved it out of Land Lot 78, owned by Reuben Cone, and into Land Lot 77, owned by Samuel Mitchell.

The land was then secured from Mitchell by former Governor Lumpkin on behalf of the state. Along with the right of way through his land, on July 11, 1842, Mitchell donated five acres for a town square at no cost to the state. The donation of the land was said by Lumpkin to be "actuated by patriotic motives," although Mitchell had also just dramatically increased the value of his property in Land Lot 77. These five acres would become the first cleared area in Atlanta, called the State Square, and later the location of the Union Station between Pryor Street and Central Avenue.

The president of the Monroe Railroad protested to the current governor, Charles James McDonald (governor from 1839 to 1843). The Western and Atlantic was then ordered to suspend contracting for the work until the matter was sufficiently examined by the state legislature. In later testimony, the chief engineer of the Western and Atlantic, Charles Garnett, declared that he "personally directed the location of the southern terminus of the

A view from 1864 looking Northwest across the State Square showing the depot that was built around 1853. *Library of Congress.*

Western and Atlantic Railroad. Mr. F.C. Arms, my assistant, did locate the square to be occupied by the depot and other buildings on the lands of Samuel Mitchell, and located the right of way for the railroad through said lands."

After an investigation, Governor Macdonald was satisfied that the change had been made legitimately and the final location of the depot was moved. The construction of the state road continued. Lumpkin, Garnett and Mitchell worked together to lay out the new town and parcel out lots that would soon go up for sale.

Together, Mitchell and Garnett decided to honor their friend Lumpkin with the name of the new town they had laid out. Lumpkin's daughter was named Martha, and they would call the new place Marthasville.

There has been a lingering, often unspoken suspicion that the changes to the location of the terminus and the naming of the town were motivated by some kind of shenanigans and those shenanigans may have involved Wilson Lumpkin, the former governor of Georgia. The perplexing choices made by Garnett and Lumpkin weren't finished with the moving to the location of the terminus. The layout of the square and the streets around it has drawn the curiosity and suspicion of many of historians as well. The State Square was not a square at all. It was a rectangle, and instead of facing north and south as one would normally expect, the Square was laid out with its longer side running northeast to southwest. The Marthasville streets were then laid out around the State Square in the same fashion, with the north–south streets running off to the northeast and southeast and the east–west streets laid out northwest and southeast. Just outside of the primary land lots owned by Mitchell, Cone and Ivy, the streets return to a north–south and east–west orientation so that there are multiple bends in many of the city's main streets. The generally accepted reasoning for this crooked orientation of the city came from Jonathan Norcross:

> The reason why the streets are so crooked is, that every man built on his land just to suit himself. The charter that was broken up by Cousin John and those associated with him (a proposed charter for Atlanta in 1846 that was quashed), provided for the appointment of commissioners to lay out the streets, but they were not allowed, or would not exercise their duties, and so everyone built upon his own hind just as he pleased. There were only just a few that believed there would ever be a town here at all. That was one reason why the commissioners would not act—they did not think it a matter of much importance. Governor Crawford did not believe that there would

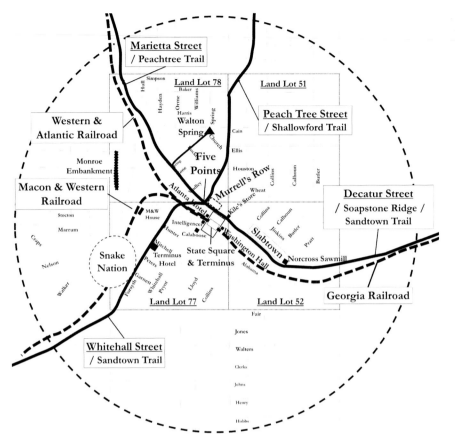

Atlanta in 1853 showing the land lots and the diagonal orientation of the major streets and the State Square. *Sketch by the author using sources from Library of Congress.*

ever be a city here, and Colonel Long of the State Road said that Atlanta would never be anything but a wood station.

The crooked layout of the square and Atlanta's streets is the key to unraveling the entire mystery of the moving of the terminus. The real mystery is why there has never been a full explanation for the change in the location of the terminus in 1842 and why it was never explained at the time by Lumpkin or Garnett or anyone else. It was done for obvious, valid, logical reasons. Perhaps the real reasons were considered somehow lacking integrity or there was a concern that the engineers would have been seen as not having done their jobs adequately, because the truth is that Native Americans laid out the city of Atlanta.

Most of the work to closely understand the landscape that would become Atlanta was already performed for the railroads' engineers by the time they began staking out the railroads. A thousand years or more before any Americans arrived in the area, using only their intuition about how best to travel through the landscape, Native Americans had already identified the spot as an important one in the landscape, the one destined to be the location of Atlanta. They also identified the location that would become the downtown area and laid out the orientation of what would be its major streets and the State Square. They also identified the best courses through the landscape that would become large sections of the railroads and how they would approach and meet in Atlanta. These were not the Creeks, but people who lived in the area long before the Creeks or the arrival of any Europeans in America.

The change to the terminus made by Garnett and Lumpkin made its location more consistent with how the land was already being used. The previous location was alongside the trail to Marietta. The terminus would now be placed at the intersection of the Peachtree Trail and the Sandtown Trail, the two main thoroughfares passing through the area at that time. This would make the State Square more likely to develop into the center of town as the natural spot through which people were already traveling. There was already a precedent for laying out a town center over top of a major intersection of trails in nearby Decatur, where the old Dekalb County Courthouse sits directly on top of the intersection of the Shallowford Trail and the Sandtown Trail.

This conscious choice made by Garnett is confirmed by the fact that after moving the terminus he went on to lay out the streets and the square consistently with the area's major trails. The move from one land lot to another was incidental to the choice, not motivated by greed or ego. The Sandtown Trail generally runs in a northeast to southwesterly direction from Decatur to Sandtown. At the location Garnett and Lumpkin chose, the Peachtree Trail runs off to the northwest. Garnett laid out the streets on Mitchell's property consistent with this northeast–southeast by southeast–northwest orientation. Using these main roads as a baseline, it was natural to lay out the other streets along this northeast by southwest orientation. As time passed, people naturally put their businesses and homes along these major thoroughfares. Roads that were laid out farther from this intersection went back to a north–south by east–west orientation and thereby made the roads crooked as Jonathan Norcross pointed out. The mistake in this was on the part of those who

An 1864 view looking northwest where the Western and Atlantic (*right*) and the Macon and Western (*left*) met in Atlanta. *Library of Congress.*

shifted back to the north–south and east–west orientation. That is why the roads are crooked.

The correctness of this choice was confirmed once again by the arrival of the railroads. When the Georgia Railroad, the Western and Atlantic Railroad and the Macon and Western Railroad arrived at their intersection in Atlanta, they each also followed one of these trails. Like Garnett, the chief engineers for the other railroads could find no better course for the tracks than the ones that had been found thousands of years earlier. The Western and Atlantic's tracks followed the Marietta trail to the Chattahoochee. The Macon and Western Railroad followed the Sandtown Trail southwest out of the downtown Atlanta area and then bent farther south at the old Newnan Road still following the local trails. The Georgia Railroad followed the Sandtown Trail northeast out of Atlanta to Decatur.

The railroad engineers did, in fact, do their jobs well. They surveyed the entire area and its hills and found the best courses to run tracks through area according to the specifications they had for changes in elevation and the sharpness of any turns so that the tracks could meet up smoothly and easily. It just turned out that they were unable to make any significant improvements on what the Native Americans had already done.

15

Pathways in the Woods that Became Downtown Atlanta

Oft and anon, would they strike in their wanderings, a beaten path, or trail, and eagerly followed it, but their expeditions would only lead to some spring used by the railroad hands a few years before. One of the springs was near where the Forsyth Street bridge was built years and years afterwards; the other was the famous Walton Spring.
—William Stafford Irvine

The area that would become Atlanta was crisscrossed by several major trails created by the Native Americans who had lived in the area for thousands of years before the Atlanta pioneers. Many of the most important trails are visible today because they formed the major roads through the area.

Walton Spring Trail (Spring Street)

The trail leading to Walton Spring is commemorated by Spring Street. Walton Spring was on the property of councilman Anderson W. Walton, being original city lot No. 120 in Land Lot 78. Walton's lot had a frontage of 135 feet on the northeast side of Walton Street and the northwest corner of Spring Street and ran back 459 feet in a northeasterly direction almost to Cain Street. The spring itself was on the rear of the lot in low ground. Its location is now marked by a city park.

Sandtown Trail (Sycamore Street/College Avenue/Decatur Street/DeKalb Avenue)

Long before there was Atlanta, the largest and oldest settlement in the area was Sandtown, and if you wanted to get there you needed to take the Sandtown Trail. The trail runs west from Stone Mountain along the ridge where the Georgia Railroad is now (also the location of the old Stone Mountain wagon road). It then enters the area of Decatur along Sycamore Street, then passes out on Atlanta Avenue and follows the location of the railroad and the Eastern Continental Divide—College Avenue to DeKalb Avenue to La France Street to Decatur Street to Five Points in Atlanta.

At Five Points, the trail turns down Forsyth Street along Whitehall Street then along Cascade Avenue, then Cascade Road and then to Sandtown right around the point where Wilson Creek and Utoy Creek enters the Chattahoochee near Buzzard's Roost Island. The trail eventually reaches Echota in North Georgia, the capital of the Cherokee Nation.

Peachtree Trail (Peachtree Road)

One of the easiest trails to locate around Atlanta, like the Hightower/Etowah Trail, is the Peachtree Trail. This is because it is now called Peachtree Road. This trail forks in Buckhead with one fork running through following Peachtree Road and the other following Paces Ferry Road and Moore's Mill Road to the location of Standing Peachtree where Peachtree Creek meets the Chattahoochee. The Peachtree Trail passes through DeKalb County along the high ground where the Norfolk Southern Railway is now located. Another part of this trail left Five Points over the ridge where Marietta Street is now located and passed to Standing Peachtree.

Soapstone Ridge Trail (Bouldercrest Road and Flat Shoals Road)

There is another important trail that passes through Decatur and leads from Soapstone Ridge and the headwaters of the South River (South Fork of the Ocmulgee River) to Five Points. It runs along Bouldercrest Road and

A view looking South down Whitehall Street (also known as the Sandtown Trail) in 1864. *Library of Congress.*

Flat Shoals Road and connects with the Stone Mountain–Sandtown Trail somewhere before reaching Five Points. On the plaque attached to the old DeKalb County Courthouse, it is marked as the Sandtown Trail but should be distinguished from the Stone Mountain–Sandtown Trail that runs along Rockbridge Road.

FAYETTEVILLE TRAIL
(PANTHERSVILLE ROAD AND FAYETTEVILLE ROAD)

There is almost certainly another trail that runs from the Soapstone Ridge area of Atlanta to Fayetteville, though there is no known documentation of it. An 1864 map of Georgia shows a road that runs in this direction, and most of these roads were indeed created along Indian trails. The likely course of this one is along Panthersville Road to Bouldercrest Road then on to Mt. Zion Boulevard and then Fayetteville Road.

SHALLOWFORD TRAIL
(CLAIREMONT AVENUE AND LAVISTA ROAD)

Another very important location that was a common waypoint for people passing through Decatur, usually headed into Cherokee territory, was the shallow ford in the Chattahoochee.

From the old DeKalb County Courthouse, the Shallowford Trail runs north on Clairemont Avenue, a slight right onto to Lavista Road, then a slight left onto Oakgrove Road until it becomes Briarcliff Road. There, it finally gets back to its original name from the settlement era of Shallowford Road. It then runs over Peachtree Creek, crosses Peachtree Road between Chamblee and Doraville and then reaches the Chattahoochee at the old Shallow Ford around two miles south of Roswell, where it intersects with the Hightower/Etowah Trail.

There is some confusion over where the trail passes to after this point. The best authority on the topic, Carl Hudgins, believed the trail leaves Shallowford Road where it intersects with Buford Highway, crosses over that road and passes northward toward the foot of the hill there. It then turns to the right and crosses Peachtree Trail at the Presbyterian Cemetery north of

Chamblee. It then coincides with Peachtree Road. It turns to the left some and runs toward what is now Chamblee Dunwoody Road. From there, it passes through Dunwoody and meets up with the Hightower/Etowah Trail east of Roswell Road.

From Five Points, one can join the Shallowford Trail by joining it in Decatur using the Sandtown trail or walking up the Peachtree Trail and picking it up at a fork in Buckhead that ran toward Piedmont Park and then to Briarcliff Road.

South of the Historic Dekalb Courthouse, the trail was called the Indian Springs Trail because it leads to the Indian Springs plantation owned by the chief of the Lower Creeks, William McIntosh. It runs along what is now McDonough Street and, at some point, probably overlaps with Candler Road.

Hightower/Etowah Trail
(The Eastern Border of DeKalb County)

The most historically important trail in the Atlanta region is the Hightower Trail. After people began to settle the area and as treaties were establishing the division of land between the Creeks to the south and Cherokees to the north, the Hightower Trail was often used to define the boundary.

With only two exceptions, we now call these trails by the names given to them by English-speaking settlers. The Hightower Trail is (sort of) one of these exceptions, and the other is the Echota. Several early maps use the name Hightower interchangeably with the word Etowah when referring to the river and other landmarks. The word is derived from the Cherokee word Ita-Wa, the name for the people that once lived in the Etowah mound village. Although it is most commonly called the Hightower, the more proper name for the trail is the Etowah Trail.

Unlike some of the other trails, it's easy to locate where much of the Hightower Trail is relative to Atlanta because it forms the northern boundary between DeKalb and Gwinnett Counties. It descends into the Atlanta region from the Etowah River in the north. It then crosses the Chattahoochee River at the Shallow Ford located two miles south of Roswell. A section of the old trail crosses Roswell Road just south of the river and is still called the Hightower Trail.

From there, it runs a meandering route following the DeKalb County border along Dunwoody Club Road, part of Winter's Chapel Road, along

This rock in Southwest Atlanta was carved by the Creeks to resemble an owl and is thought to mark the location of a trail leading to Sandtown. *Photo by the author.*

the southern border of Graves Park and across the Heritage Golf Links. It then crosses Lawrenceville Road just northeast of Tucker, and it then passes on to a small part of Old Tucker Road and on to Stone Mountain. It crosses the Yellow River at the old rock bridge, now Rockbridge Road, and passes on to a section that still bears the name just southeast of there. From there, the trail passes High Shoals on the Apalachee River and goes on toward Augusta. Along its course, there are historical markers in several places, including the point at which it crosses Lawrenceville Highway and Peachtree Road just north of Doraville.

THE STONE MOUNTAIN WALKUP TRAIL

There is one trail that has almost certainly been in constant use longer than any of the others and is still in daily use today. We know that it was being used long before the Creeks came here. It almost undoubtedly has been used since the first human beings set foot in the Southeast. This is the one that ascends the western slope of Stone Mountain. Stone Mountain was exposed above the landscape about fifteen million years ago and has looked almost the same during all that time. If you were the first hunter to venture into new hunting grounds and noticed that giant rock rising above the trees, visible from miles away, would you be able to resist approaching it and walking to the top?

THE STANDING PEACHTREE/SANDTOWN TRAIL

Another trail runs down the banks of the Chattahoochee to take travelers between the two Indian towns of Standing Peachtree and Sandtown.

16

John Thrasher Departs, Sarah Carlisle Arrives to Old Terminus

John Thrasher and his crews finished the Monroe embankment in 1841. Thrasher's net proceeds from the work were about $10,000 after his partner Johnson's share and his other expenses. As a young man just starting out, this was more money than he ever expected to have. He found himself uncomfortable with his own success. He said he had more money "than should be in the keeping of one man." In the case of Thrasher, this was not false humility. He divided much of his wealth among his family members, including many of his vast array of cousins. He felt far less lucky when it came to his investments around the embankment.

When the terminus moved, John Thrasher became the owner of one hundred acres of land built near a now useless embankment and about a quarter of a mile or so distant from the location of the planned depot in the new town that would not be called Deantown but Marthasville.

"That was my ruin," he said:

> *I bought one hundred acres of land with the expectation that the Macon road would stop up by the State road shops* [Thrasher was saying this after the state road shops had been located near the original spot for Terminus], *and when I found that the road was going down here, I was very much enraged, and sold out my interest in that hundred acres for four dollars an acre, although it was about one-half of what I gave for it. I did not think the property would ever be worth anything out there, and I sold out and went to Griffin. Nobody looked for the*

The Monroe Embankment as it looks in 2020 under the parking decks of the Georgia World Congress Center. *Photo by the author.*

development to move off to the east. I had made up my mind that there would be at least half a dozen stores in Deantown, and that it was going to be a right smart place.

The land that was originally intended to become the terminus was back under the control of Reuben Cone. It became unattended but not completely abandoned. A few of the Irish families who had come to Terminus with bright prospects of hope for the future stayed in the little shacks Thrasher had built, with their slightly used wooden floors. They were jobless now. Many had no resources or means to relocate. They stuck it out and took over what was left of Terminus until they were encountered by another pair of newcomers who came to settle in Marthasville, Willis and Sarah Carlisle.

Sarah described their arrival eloquently:

My father moved to Georgia in 1828. Later, they moved to Marietta where I was married in 1841. Rev. Josiah Burke, who performed the ceremony, advised my husband to move to Terminus, as he said it would someday be a large place. We took his advice, and one warm day in June [Willis and Sarah Carlisle came to Terminus from Marietta on June 17, 1842] *we started out on our journey. Not greater was the fire and enthusiasm that coursed the veins of those who long ago turned their faces toward the California wilds in search of gold than was that of this young couple as they started to win the goal (or gold) at Terminus.*

As we, with our wagons and worldly effects, reached our destination, a rude structure which we had procured from Judge Cone, of Decatur, as a dwelling, we found, to our consternation, that it was occupied, and, what was more, by rude people who refused to vacate. There we were, alone, thrust out into the wilderness without shelter, neighbor or friend. It was the only available shelter for miles around, having been built by Mr. John Thrasher (known as "Cousin John") and used years before as a commissary for the old "Monroe Road" hands. It was situated on Marietta Road, in front of the present First Presbyterian Church. The families occupying it were Irish, employed to grade the road, and seemed to be fixtures. We began looking about us for shelter, until we could notify Judge Cone, and finally found an old dilapidated shanty in which cattle had found refuge, and here we camped. After some delay, we obtained possession of shanty number one, which, for comfort, was little better than that we had just vacated.

Where the Irish family squatting in the commissary went, we do not know. The only person the Carlisles made regular contact with during this time was Tom Shivers, who drove the stagecoach back and forth between Decatur and Marietta. Formerly, the stage road between these two towns went out west from Decatur, passing by what is today Piedmont Park along the Echota Trail, crossing Peachtree Road to Montgomery Ferry, then northwest to Marietta, but now that prospective railroads were being centered at Terminus, the route had been changed.

Other former workers on the railroad were trickling into the area as the construction progressed in other nearby parts of the state. The previously genteel, quiet county of DeKalb was becoming disorderly. The DeKalb Grand Jury for 1842 wrote,

> *Viewing the amount of bill of indictment which have come before us, although it is with pain that we have to take notice to such an occurrence, as having been heretofore not to be complained of. We recommend that all civil officers be vigilant in the discharge of their duties in the suppression of all of those petty matters that have to consume the time of grand juries and that of the court, resulting from personal broils....*
>
> *We are apprised that former grand jurors of our county have before expressed their opinions with regard to the currency and the effects it has produced, and would recommend still as a proper course to pursue that the debtor class be vigilant, industrious and economical, and by pursuing this course those days of plenty which we so much lament will ere long return to our much distressed country. And also would recommend forbearance on the part of those who have it in their power to distress others, so far as is consistent with justice to themselves, their families and fellowmen.*

Translated to twenty-first-century-style speech, these two paragraphs are saying first, the court docket in Decatur was being clogged with daily infractions that they felt were relatively minor and personal and they would like local law enforcement to try to handle these rather than send them to the court. The second paragraph is saying the court recognized the poor economic condition of the country and encouraged the poorer citizens to continue to work hard while it exhorted the lending citizens to be patient with debts.

17

THE FIRST TRAIN ROLLS OUT
FROM THE TERMINUS

Toward the end of 1842, things started to look a little more optimistic. While Marthasville was being laid out into crooked lots, and the State Square was still being laid out on its crooked angles, the little town reached a milestone. Under the energetic supervision of former governor Lumpkin and Chief Engineer Garnett, the tracks of the Western and Atlantic Railroad between Marthasville and Marietta were at last completed.

All work above the Etowah River was still suspended. This point lies only about forty miles above Marietta. The day would come soon when the tracks would be there. A bill would then need to be passed in the legislature to continue the project. As Lumpkin well knew, despite reaching Marietta, the completion of the Western and Atlantic would still require enormous funding and effort. Even he probably had no idea just how long it would take. The entire Western and Atlantic line between Atlanta and Chattanooga would not be completed until May 9, 1850. In the end, the construction of the Western and Atlantic Railroad cost the taxpayers of Georgia $3,680,165.88.

Lumpkin had been promoting the railroad to Georgians for most of his career and knew how to use an event to do so. Any enthusiasm for railroads he could generate among taxpayers would be enormously valuable in convincing the legislature to vote to complete the project. The world's greatest showman, P.T. Barnum, had just begun his career and introduced his first major hoax, the Feejee Mermaid, in 1842. It was a stuffed fish with the head of a monkey that Barnum presented as a real animal. Governor Lumpkin, disbursing agent for the Western and Atlantic, may have taken a page out of the book of the legendary promoter to draw attention back to railroads in Georgia. He created a mass media event of Barnum-like proportions, focused on the state's railroads and put them back on the public's mind and closer to their hearts.

Plans were established for a great celebration that would honor the first train to roll out of Atlanta on the new Western and Atlantic rails, and what better night for a grand celebration than to do it on Christmas Eve? There was one problem though. The new tracks from Marthasville connected to Marietta—and that was it. As it was put at the time, the railroad "didn't start nowhere and didn't go nowhere."

How could one roll a train out of Marthasville without a track to get the train there in the first place? There was certainly no factory in Marthasville or in Marietta to create a new locomotive. Even a very small steam locomotive weighs several tons, not an easy thing to move under horsepower.

Nevertheless, that is what they did, and the solution was genius. It became the real event that vastly extended and intensified the spotlight on Georgia's train tracks for its citizens, far more than the Christmas Eve excursion itself. P.T. Barnum would have been impressed. Lumpkin purchased a small locomotive for the Western and Atlantic from the Georgia Railroad where it had been in service since 1837. It was named the Florida.

The Florida was brought to the end of the Georgia line in Madison, and there, it was loaded onto a sturdy wagon pulled by sixteen mules. They would then haul the locomotive slowly down the stagecoach road to the terminus, showing off the marvel of the time to crowds along the way. Most of the people along the route had never seen a machine of any kind like this one. It must have made an incredible sight as the mule train and its locomotive plodded slowly along the sixty miles past Covington, through Panthersville and Decatur and finally into Marthasville. A single passenger car and a freight car were also purchased from the State Penitentiary in Milledgeville and brought over land in similar fashion to meet up with the locomotive.

As the mules trudged through the forests and towns, the event took on the character of a whistle-stop tour. People traveled miles to watch and cheer it rolling by. One of the wide-eyed children who got to see the Florida as it passed was G.G. Smith, who provided many vivid descriptions of Atlanta during its earliest days. He was only about six years old at the time and would have seen it as it passed Oxford, Georgia.

By the time the train approached Marthasville, the roads on all sides of the terminus were clogged with wagons. The Florida and its cars must have arrived sometime around the beginning of December 1843. It probably

Arrival of the locomotive Florida at Terminus, 1842. *Atlanta History Center.*

took a number of days to get them properly placed on the tracks and hooked up, the anticipation growing by the hour. The legislative act that suspended work on the Western and Atlantic north of the Etowah River was repealed on December 22, 1843, while the Florida was still drawing crowds in Atlanta and preparing to christen the tracks between Atlanta and Marietta. Lumpkin had pulled off a huge success for the Western and Atlantic.

A terrific ball was planned in Marietta to await their arrival on Christmas Eve. With continued construction of the tracks now confirmed, it was bound to be a lively celebration. Invitations went out to a carefully chosen list of influential guests who would have the great honor of being the first to depart Marthasville by rail, including several politicians who would speak in support of railroads at the party in Marietta.

By the most reliable accounts, the engineer of this first trip out of Marthasville was Jim Rustin. As Engineer Rustin prepared to leave, he yelled out, "Now, boys! I want you to give me a good shove! I think when I get started I can keep going!" When he finally began coaxing the Florida slowly forward, the whooshing of the steam was drowned away by the roar of the cheering crowd and the firing of guns in celebration.

Thomas Cruselle was among the jubilant Marthasvillians and visitors who helped to push the locomotive out of the station on its journey down the new tracks and then ran behind to see it off. Several of the well-wishers tumbled over one another as the train pulled out. Engineer Rustin had to make one scheduled stop along the way to Marietta to allow a few passengers to step down and walk across the bridge over the Chattahoochee. Not everyone aboard fully trusted the strength of these new tracks to cross them safely over the water.

One of those lucky few was a very young Rebecca Latimer, who grew up to become quite a notable person in America. Later, as Rebecca Latimer Felton, she would have the great distinction to become the first woman to ever serve in the U.S. Congress, though only for one day. In 1842, she was just a seven-year-old farm girl witnessing the technological marvel of the time roll past her front door:

The civil engineer of the Georgia road made his headquarters at our home off and on for perhaps eighteen months. The progress of both undertakings was a topic of daily conversation where I could wonder and also listen. When the state railroad was able to lay down rails from Atlanta, then known as Marthasville, to Marietta, twenty miles, the engine, freight car and passenger coach were hauled…over the stage line, and the wonderful new cars were halted in the big road in front of my home.…It was decided to celebrate the opening of the state road by an excursion to Marietta from Marthasville with a big ball at the latter place and considerable speech-making from the politicians. It was the first adventure of that sort in the Southern States and broke the ice for internal public improvements. My parents were invited by the beloved civil engineers. I was included, a tot of seven years, and I could now paint scenes, if I was an artist, with distinct remembrance of what I saw on that great trip.

The future Capitol of Georgia then had one building, the rough plank depot, with a shed room equipped with a fireplace where all sorts of good liquor could be bought, etc.

It was a cold day in the late fall and my father and mother, with my small self, reachtd [sic] Thompson's Hotel in Decatur, where the excursionists assembled and where a fine dinner was provided. It was a six-mile drive to Marthasville and conveyances were in demand. We were delighted when Maria Gertrude Kyle took a seat in our barouche on my mother's invitation, as she was a well-known as authoress and poetess, in our few Georgia papers. She had lately married and her new clothes interested me, and I was even more interested to see her dance that night in some of the new sort of dances, different from the Virginia Reel and cotillions that I had been accustomed to, in our own home, by tourists who traveled from Savannah and Augusta to Nashville, Tenn., and regions beyond, either in a stage coach or private carriages. The supper was handed to us as the people sat on benches around the Marietta ball room. Some people had syllabub strong with Madeira wine, but I had a wine glass of jelly and a spoon with which to dip it out.

I soon had enough of the frolic and was put to sleep in a bed, already a foot deep with shawls, capes and bonnets. The joyful folks danced all night. There were relays of fiddlers to keep the tunes going. I remember I thought I had been awake all the time because the music and the calling of dance figures and the dancers' feet seemed to be going on until daylight in the morning.

The trip homeward was as dull as the going had been hilarious, but I have always taken satisfaction in the thought that I was a trip passenger on the very first passenger train that ever left the Union Depot in the present City of Atlanta. Judge Warner, the grandfather of Judge Warner Hill, of the Supreme Court, was on board with his little daughter, now

The Pioneer of the Chicago and Northwestern Railroad probably looks very similar to the Florida, the first locomotive to steam out of Atlanta. *Library of Congress.*

Mrs. Hill. So far as we know she and I are the only two known to be living, and fellow travelers on that momentous occasion when a railroad was adventuring into Cherokee Georgia where the Cherokee Indians had been living only ten years before.

Sadly, the Florida itself was not preserved to take its rightful place as an important relic to the history of Atlanta, and we have no specific descriptions of it. Lore tells that it was a "kettle dome equipped with a single pair of drivers and a four-wheel lead truck." It would have looked very similar to the Pioneer, the first locomotive of the Chicago and Northwestern Railway.

18

FOUNDING MARTHASVILLE

The struggling enthusiasm for railroads was rekindled. Most of the energy that followed focused on connecting the Georgia railroads to Memphis, Vicksburg and Nashville. The Western and Atlantic reached Dalton in July 1847, and on December 1, 1849, service began between Atlanta and Chattanooga, although the Chetoogeta Mountain had not yet been tunneled. Until the tunnel was opened, passengers would disembark the train on one side of the mountain and then carry their luggage over to the other side of the mountain and board a different train. The connection to Memphis was finished much later.

In 1845, the legislatures of Alabama, Mississippi and Georgia chartered the South Western Railroad to run from Georgia to West Point and the Southern Railroad to run from West Point to Vicksburg. The legislature of Tennessee supported a line from Chattanooga to Nashville. The Nashville and Chattanooga line was commissioned in late 1845.

The little town of Marthasville was officially incorporated by Governor Crawford on December 23, 1843. For the first time, the place that would become Atlanta had a city government. Its first commissioners were a contractor for the railroad, a man who owned a boardinghouse that had been built by the railroad and two recently arrived grocers. One of them dealt mainly in food while the other dealt mainly in alcohol. Each of them could be seen as an archetype for how the population of the town was developing: merchants, railroad workers, hotels and drinkers.

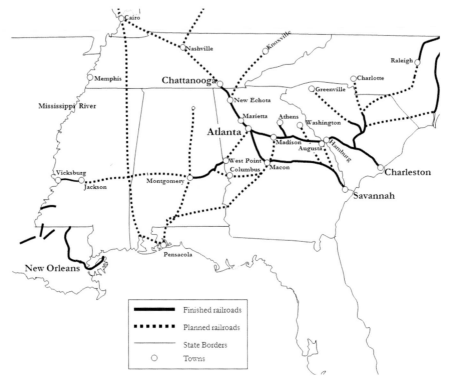

The Southern railroad network in 1856 showing how Atlanta connected Savannah and Charleston to the Mississippi River. *Sketch by the author using sources from Library of Congress.*

Attention toward the little burg was now growing. The rails made their slow progression across Georgia soil. Of those who constructed them, some stayed. Some settled in Marthasville risking their prospects against what was to come. More often though, they stayed because the same scenarios played themselves out over and over again. Limited work enticed new arrivals. Those jobs ended. They then became stranded without employment, money, assistance or any prospects of changing their situation.

The population of poor, unemployed laborers continued to swell. These poor, stranded, increasingly desperate and half-wild people without prospects became the central character of the new city. Marthasville became hard and muddy. It began to look and act like more and more like the frontier town it essentially was.

The new city commission had neither the wherewithal nor the desire to rein in the increasingly bad behavior of the newcomers. Nor did it develop Marthasville in any other sensible way. It tried to collect taxes for new streets and other improvements, but the citizens simply refused to pay. Thomas Martin asserted, "The first government was by all accounts a 'kangaroo' government. The attempt to gather taxes was a complete waste and the city continued with no financial resources."

With no resources supporting the town, there was no way to enforce city legislation and, therefore, no penalties for this refusal to pay city taxes. Clearly not everyone wanted to see the town government strengthen and develop. When unemployed, the professions that might otherwise be outlawed, like gambler, bootlegger or prostitute, were usually the most attainable occupations in which to try and eke out a living.

19

The Arrival of Jonathan Norcross, Atlanta's Most Important Early Citizen

S ometime in 1844, the person who had the most overall influence on early Atlanta came ambling to town on horseback. A more shrewd and calculating person probably had never entered Marthasville prior to that day. His influence over the formation of the town was monumental. Virtually nothing of importance happened in Atlanta or Marthasville for the next ten years that didn't have the close involvement of Jonathan Norcross.

Apart from the obsessive devotion and energy he applied to the organization and promotion of this new city, Norcross was a person of remarkable intellect and wide-ranging talents. He found success in several areas through his long career in Atlanta and elsewhere as an inventor, machinist, proprietor, merchant, investor, schoolteacher, politician and eventually president of one of Atlanta's railroads. He even wrote several well-accepted scholarly pieces during his lifetime. He wrote a book called *The History of Democracy* in 1837, and it contains a deep and accurate understanding of the changes to federal financial policy that precipitated the crash. Norcross properly and boldly put the majority of the blame for the crash of 1837 with Andrew Jackson and said of the president, "He was a man of limited education, limited political information, and of a stubborn and vindictive disposition."

As he was a former mayor and a man who lived to the ripe old age of ninety, there are many pictures of Jonathan Norcross. In all of them, one gets the same sense of the man. He looks like he is devouring the camera with his eyes. This is probably the same intelligent, intense glare with which he regarded people he met. He always wore a beard, but beneath it one

Jonathan Norcross. The most influential person of Atlanta's antebellum era. *Atlanta History Center.*

can see the strong chin jutting forward under teeth clenched with purpose. There was probably no one who ever had any question whether Jonathan Norcross meant what he said.

Norcross was a unionist. He never supported the tenets of secession. He greatly regretted that the Civil War had not been avoided and blamed it on the philosophies of the Democratic party at the time:

> *No other than a Democratic party could ever have brought on the great calamity of a great civil war in this country. Hence the just conclusion is, that but for the Democratic party, the great problem of slavery in this country would probably have been solved, and universal freedom have been ultimately established by peaceable means.*

Norcross was also a man with a famously strict moral code that guided every aspect of his life and his views of society. He was born the second son of a Yankee reverend, Jesse Norcross, and Nancy Gaubert of Charlestown, Maine. His adherence to the high moral standards with which he had been raised was exemplified through many actions of his life but perhaps most by the fact his son Virgil chose to become a Baptist preacher like Jonathan's father.

He got a good education in Maine and worked as a millwright when still a boy. He left home at just sixteen or so and worked for a sugar plantation in Cuba setting up mills and other machinery. Around 1826, he came back to the United States and added to his education with a course of lectures on mechanics at the Franklin Institute in Philadelphia for two years. While there, he published some of his first scholarly articles. An essay he published on mercantile integrity received a good amount of praise. The assimilation of his aspirations for business and his moral upbringing were becoming apparent.

Around 1833, he headed south. He first lived in North Carolina working as a teacher and then made his way to Georgia in 1835. While still working as a teacher in Augusta, he somehow was put in charge of a large investment into lumber interests in south Georgia made by a group of northern investors. This gave him direct exposure to the opportunities the railroads were creating in lumber. This gave Norcross ideas about the next part of his career and brought him to Marthasville.

He was only thirty-six when he arrived but had already been on his own gaining education and experience and showing great potential for about twenty years. He appeared with a very clear idea in mind for a business niche that was likely to pay him handsomely. The railroad needed two things in vast quantities: wood and iron. Norcross put his experience with machinery and mills in Maine and Cuba to good use. He first put up a sawmill at the corner of Decatur and Pratt Streets and immediately began a contract with the Georgia Railroad to supply the string timber, sills and crossties the railroad needed. After a few months, he built a home near his mill on the corner of Decatur and Pratt Streets.

According to G.G. Smith, "The young city was in the woods with only one brick house in it." The area around Norcross's mill was densely wooded and marshy. Cattle would often be found mired in the mud just outside his door. Stately oaks and scrubby pines leaned over and canopied all the town's trails and roads. Some travelers through Georgia around this time reported they could stretch out their arms while on horseback and touch the trees on either side for much of the journey. So, when Norcross and W.H. Forsyth, his sawyer, went to gather the fodder to run the sawmill they needed but walk a few feet out the front door.

Norcross's sawmill used a new design of his own invention. It had an upright saw that could be operated with the power of just one horse walking in a circle. He visited Washington around 1844 to patent his new design but found that another inventor had recently patented a similar one. He continued to sell the concept as his own though and was successful in licensing it to a few other millwrights.

Norcross also opened a store in 1845. Always innovative with machinery, he was the first person in Atlanta or Marthasville to automate the processing of corn. Corn was still in high demand to be shipped out of Charleston and Savannah to Ireland to try to relieve the famine. Norcross employed a dozen people (at twenty cents per day) to package and prepare the corn for shipping.

Along with Jonathan Norcross, another man arrived in Marthasville for the first time in 1844 who would also have an enormous effect on its future. A young lieutenant named William Tecumseh Sherman made a survey of Marthasville and its nearby regions on behalf of the U.S. Army. This familiarity with the landscape must have been useful when Sherman returned as a general in the winter of 1864 to destroy the railroads and burn a large portion of the city to the ground.

20

SLABTOWN AND MURRELL'S ROW

Norcross and his sawmill became the foundation supporting Marthasville's first well-known neighborhood. It was called Slabtown. Slabtown came to be out of the fairly noble intentions of Jonathan Norcross when he settled in Marthasville, but it developed an infamous reputation very soon after that.

When a sawmill processes a tree into lumber, it first cuts away the pieces on the outside of the tree to produce a smoother, squared beam. These outer pieces that often include the outer bark of the tree, are discarded. These discarded outer pieces of the tree are called slabs. With steady demand from the Georgia Railroad and others, Norcross's mill was cranking out a large pile of slabs every day. He sold these slabs to people at low prices or just discarded them outside the mill, where they were free for anyone to take away. Most of the houses for several blocks around the mill became a mishmash of homemade structures built using these slabs, some with the bark still exposed toward the exterior. Hence, this was Slabtown.

Initially, the creation of Slabtown was viewed with a level of pride by the more sophisticated residents in Marthasville. It demonstrated a feeling of altruism and generosity toward its new citizens befitting the civilized burg they wanted to create. It showed there was opportunity in Marthasville and grew the citizenry that the merchants needed for business. A newcomer with nothing could come to Marthasville, build a shanty made of slabs, set up residence and look for work. Over time, Slabtown became viewed less

These are shacks erected by Federal troops on the State Square in 1864, but they are made of slabs and probably closely resemble the shacks of Slabtown. *Library of Congress.*

and less with a charitable heart. As petty crime continued to grow, fingers were more and more often pointed toward Slabtown. It became one of the areas known to house the usual suspects for the city's daily misconduct.

By the mid-1840s, Marthasville was beginning to bustle. The main population growth of the muddy, little town continued to be transient or unemployed railroad workers. Many were immigrants like the Irish families Mrs. Carlisle had encountered squatting in the old Thrasher and Johnson store. A large portion of them were young men on their own for the first time in their lives, seeking fortune but with no particular ideas or plan for finding it.

Left to their own judgment, without employment and any kind of planning or structure to the new city, the new citizens of Marthasville filled their time with activities typical to an American frontier town. There were soon more drinking establishments, brothels and gambling rooms in the city than there were stores. Crime became rampant, and there was no visible possibility or even firm resolve to fight it.

Nearby, in the more established, more genteel town of Decatur, the county's leaders were becoming frustrated with their loud, new neighbors. They made this frustration clear in a statement of the DeKalb Grand Jury

An 1864 view looking North up Whitehall Street toward the tracks and Five Points. The building on the right is the Georgia Railroad Bank. *Library of Congress.*

in March 1844: "Vice and immorality seems to be prevailing in our County, particularly on the line of the Rail Road. We recommend all officers whose duty it is to be vigilant in bringing offenders to justice."

The epicenter of wild and wooly Marthasville was in Murrell's Row, located on the north side of Five Points. The border between the two main opposing groups in this rivalry was the railroad tracks. Henry McDaniel (governor of Georgia from 1883 to 1886) lived in Marthasville and Atlanta as a young man and played his role as a member of one of these loosely organized gangs. He recounted:

> *The boys of the town were divided then as older folks are now, by the railroad, the south side being called the Savannah side from Whitehall Street and the other side the Murrell's Row side. McDaniel was a Savannah side man and fought its fights manfully but would never aid in pummeling a Murrell's Row boy who was caught out by himself.*

The chief amusement and vehicle for gambling in Murrell's Row were the cockfights. There were several cockfighting pits there, and the battles would sometimes attract spectators and bettors in the hundreds. These activities were normally being enjoyed from sun-up to well past sun-down in the increasingly loud, steaming Five Points crossroads.

One early pioneer by the name of Thomas George Cruselle was one of the town toughs and told a strange, thrilling story to the *Atlanta Journal* in 1890 about a typical rough interaction in Murrell's Row around the cockfights:

> *Jim Toney was quite a character here then* [mid-1840s]. *He used to call himself the best judge of corn whisky and peach brandy on earth. He had queer notions about witchcraft and things like that. When a cow licks herself while she's shedding, her tongue gathers a ball of hair that she swallows. It comes up with the cud and is thrown out on the ground. Toney was afraid of the hair balls and if one was found on the place where he lived he would get away from there quick.*
>
> *I was laughing at him about his hair balls and witchcraft and he got mad. So, we fell out, and not long after, we met at a chicken fight. I had a chicken of the Bill Harwell stock, as we called it then, and Tom Shivers*

Atlanta residents about to start a cock fight. *Library of Congress.*

wanted it. I sold to him and soon afterward I found he had trimmed the chicken up and pitted him against the one that Toney had raised.

Just as I walked up Toney's chick knocked down the one I had sold Tom Shivers. With that Toney jumped up, flapping his arms like wings and crowed like a rooster.

I said nothing, and just as he got through crowing my chicken got up and struck Toney's bird, running a gaff through its head.

As my chick floored the other I raised my stick and floored Toney. When my chicken got up and showed fight, I showed fight too; I could not keep from it to save my life. I beat Toney good and it laid him up for some time.

In addition to the cockfight bets, the gambling houses along Decatur Street and centered on Murrell's Row hosted games like dice, kent and faro. By 1850, these gambling houses had become such a public nuisance that the marshal was at last ordered to "prosecute all faro dealers and gambling houses" in the city. Like most of Marthasville's early law enforcement, this seems to have been largely a ceremonial gesture or perhaps a city fundraiser. Once violators were prosecuted, the city did little to curtail their activities. Proprietors were fined and then back running their illicit games in a day or two.

Specifically, the name Murrell's Row was chosen to acknowledge the activities, other than gambling and drinking, that the people who frequented the area were known to pursue with enthusiasm. This was theft. Organized theft was a major problem for Marthasville. It was widespread, and the town's ability to curtail it was as weak as it was at collecting taxes or combatting other undesired activities. Murrell's Row was aptly named to connect it with one of the best-known thieves in early America.

John Murrell was one of the first outlaws to gain legendary status in America, like William Bonney or Bill Hickok. He became famous enough to be a central feature in Mark Twain's *Adventures of Tom Sawyer.* In the book, Injun Joe finds John Murrell's legendary treasure, which eventually falls into the hands of Huckleberry Finn and Tom Sawyer. Other stories still abound across the South about where Murrell may have stashed some of his treasure. There is a cave on the Etowah River north of Atlanta called Guy Rivers' Cave where some of Murrell's booty is said to still be hidden.

The actual John Murrell was indeed a criminal. That much is fact. Whether he was a criminal of anywhere near his legend is very doubtful. His notoriety sprang from a wildly popular book published in 1835 by a man named Virgil Stewart called the *History of the Detection, Conviction, Life and Designs of John A.*

Murrell, the Great Western Land Pirate. The author, Stewart, claimed to have fallen in with Murrell traveling on horseback. Stewart pretended to be a man looking for a horse and traveled many miles with him, getting a full recounting of the prodigious outlaw's life and crimes.

Through several anecdotes, Stewart described a series of brazen organized crimes, including horse theft, slave theft, robbery, burglary, mugging, extortion and murder that Murrell supposedly committed throughout the American South. He also described Murrell's "Mystic Clan," a wide network of more than one thousand criminals the outlaw could call on for assistance in any state or town of the Southeast. The book provides a roll call of many of the members of the alleged Mystic Clan, including many Georgians.

Some of Murrell's methods described in the book could be regarded as clever. They commonly involved misdirection and camouflage to carry out his crimes. For example, the Murrell depicted in the book was a preacher of some prowess. He would sometimes come to a town and advertise a sermon that would attract most of the residents to come out and listen. While the town was distracted and nearly empty, his accomplices would loot their houses and run off with their horses. Other times, he would set fire to one part of a town so that he could easily burglarize the other side of town while the residents dealt with the fire. The book acted as a manual for many would-be criminals of the mid-1800s.

Most alarming to southerners of the time, the book described a plan formulated by Murrell to inspire a mass slave rebellion on Christmas night 1835. Like the others, this story is almost certainly fiction, but it was widely believed to the degree it created a serious panic in several southern towns. Thirty people were hanged in Nashville, Memphis and Natchez for being believed accomplices in Murrell's plot. A mob ran all the town's gamblers out of Vicksburg, Mississippi, for their believed connection to Murrell and his Mystic Clan. Several other places formed committees to investigate and search for local accomplices of Murrell among their citizenry.

If any significant portion of the stories about Murrell are at all true, they would have occurred between 1829 and 1834. The real John Murrell was convicted as a horse thief when he was a teen and had his hand branded with *HT* as part of his punishment. He was released from prison for this crime in 1829 after serving six years. He was convicted again in 1834 for stealing slaves in Tennessee. This drew him another sentence from 1834 to 1844. The book was published during this stretch. While in prison, he admitted to his crimes and discussed them openly with other prisoners but denied the lion's share of what was written in the book. He said there was no such Mystic Clan and swore he neither committed nor participated in a murder. Those who wanted to believe the legend simply chalked this up to the conspiracy, of course. Murrell died of consumption less than a year after his release in 1844 in Pikeville, Tennessee.

After he was buried, Murrell's body was disinterred and mutilated by souvenir seekers. His head was removed and is now lost. His thumb though, has been retained and preserved. It is now in the possession of the Tennessee State Museum, undoubtedly the strangest artifact in its collection.

21

A Railroad Boom and a City Called Atlanta

The first locomotive steamed out of the terminus on Christmas Eve 1843 on the tracks of the Western and Atlantic. It was far from the first railroad project to be completed to Marthasville though. (The train could reach Marietta but go no farther.) The Georgia Railroad, the line coming from Augusta through Decatur, was the first to complete its planned line on September 14, 1845. The railroad's officers wasted no time admiring their accomplishment when there was much needed money to be made. The first train, the construction train, was sent into Marthasville that very evening. It had come from Augusta with ten cars and a load of iron for the Western and Atlantic.

William F. Adair had the honor of conducting that first train down the tracks of the Georgia Railroad and was the primary conductor on this section of the road for many years afterward. There is an Adair Street that commemorates the first engineer in Decatur located close to the tracks and the old depot (now a restaurant). Remembering his first historic run, Adair said,

> *While at Decatur, my engineer John Hopkins, was taken violently ill. My orders were positive. I must be in Marthasville that night. Nothing daunted I mounted my engine, the Kentucky, and pulled open the throttle. We rolled out of Decatur at 8 p.m., and I halted the engine right where the car shed now stands in Atlanta (the old Union Depot between Pryor and Central), a few minutes before 9 o'clock. The road being new and rough, I ran very*

slowly from Decatur to Marthasville. Having heard that the train would probably reach the town that day, a great many people had come down from the country above Marthasville to see the novel sight. Campfires were gleaming in the woods where the capital now stands. My train was allowed to stand where I had stopped it all night. The W&ARR, having a track laid one mile beyond the Chattahoochee, I ran my train out there and threw off the iron.

Adair may have had a sense of the history in which he was taking part. There is certainty that one emotion he was feeling as he arrived around nine o'clock must have been fear. It was dark during this first trip into Marthasville. These early locomotives were primitive, as Engineer William Hardman described:

We couldn't see anything. We had no whistle, no cowcatcher, and what's more, no cab! The engineer stood on his platform without any shelter of any kind, without any light ahead of him, without any steam whistle to sound a note of warning....Our brake was a long lever pole, working in the same way brakes are now used on large wagons. We had to bear down on the lever, stand on it altogether with the fireman, to stop the engine, and it locked only two wheels.

Once Adair had made his run with the construction train and confirmed the line was passable without an embarrassing derailment, a common occurrence in these early days, the first passenger train was sent through to Marthasville and arrived the next evening. As before when the Western and Atlantic sent its first train to Marietta, the officers of the Georgia Railroad and the leaders in the town of Marthasville used this as an event to highlight their success for the public.

Judge John P. King, the president of the Georgia Railroad, escorted the first train personally on board. Upon stepping down in the new village, he was met by a jubilant crowd that escorted him from the train. The public value of the event for Marthasville was very nearly spoiled when President King came very close to plunging to his death. There was a well about twenty feet deep near the terminus that had been left uncovered. In the darkness, among the crowd, King stepped into it and was narrowly rescued before falling in. Apparently, it was still left exposed after the first incident because later that night, another poor soul fell into the same well and was drowned.

With the arrival of the Georgia trains, at last Marthasville was no longer an "island city." It was connected by rail to the outside world. Trains (and the people they brought) began arriving regularly. The population boomed. Marthasville took on all the crowded, dirty aspects of the frontier town that it was. Few of these new residents had politics or business foremost in their minds. When they had any money, the majority of them focused on gambling, fighting, drinking and other forms of debauchery. According to Thomas Martin:

> After the railroad was finished, some of the laborers who had been thrown out of employment remained in the village, forming a rather disorderly and disreputable element of the population. They rendezvoused at a drinking dive kept by one of their number and spent their time largely gambling and cock fighting.

With its arrival as the first to complete their rails to Marthasville, the Georgia Railroad decided to put its permanent mark on the town. Perhaps for many reasons, some of them personal, they didn't like the name of the town. Marthasville was an homage to former governor Lumpkin, the disbursing agent for the Western and Atlantic Railroad. Lumpkin had changed the location of the terminus in 1842 and caused a great deal of additional planning and work for the other two railroads headed for the terminus, the Macon and Western (formerly Monroe) Railroad and the Georgia Railroad.

There were many in town who disliked the name of Marthasville but no one who would publicly say the fiasco over the shifting of the terminus was part of the reason. Publicly, they would say that as the depot became connected to the rest of the world and it would become a much more well-known location for travel and shipping, Marthasville was unequal to the grandeur that they foresaw in their new, growing settlement. Regardless of the reasons, the name fell into close public scrutiny in the fall of 1845.

As it turned out, it only took one person who didn't like the name of the town to effectively change it, and he did so rather easily. Richard Peters was superintendent of the Georgia Railroad and didn't want to print that Marthasville was a stop on the Georgia Railroad, so he didn't. Unable to come up with another name that he thought suitable, Superintendent Peters wrote a letter to his friend and chief engineer of the Georgia Railroad, J. Edgar Thompson, and solicited ideas. Thompson wrote back, "Eureka— Atlanta, the terminus of the Western & Atlantic Railroad—Atlantic

Chronicle and Sentinel.

AUGUSTA, GA.

MONDAY MORNING, SEPTEMBER 8.

FOR GOVERNOR:

GEORGE W. CRAWFORD.

Georgia Rail Road.

We are requested to state that the passenger trains will commence their regular trips on this road between Augusta and Atlanta—its western terminus—on Monday next, 15th inst. Fare $7—distance 172 miles. Freights for Atlanta will be received at the Augusta depot, at any time after the 10th instant.

The first use of the name "Atlanta" announcing the completion of the Georgia Railroad. Georgia Chronicle & Sentinel, *September 8, 1845*.

masculine, Atlanta feminine—a coined word and if you think it will suit, adopt it."

Peters loved the name and immediately began using it to refer to the stop on Georgia Railroad located in Marthasville. As one would expect, there were protests and complaints that the railroad had no right to change the name, but as it turned out, it did. The official name of the town was a matter of public and legislative record and remained officially Marthasville. The Georgia Railroad, though, had the right to name its depot whatever name it saw fit.

Peters and Thompson didn't care what the town was called. Their depot would be named Atlanta. The announcements of the anticipated completion of the Georgia Railroad went out on September 8, 1845, using the name Atlanta to refer to the terminus.

Soon the mail began to arrive regularly addressed to Atlanta. The town quickly became generally known by that name. The post office was the first to make the change official. It changed its name to Atlanta on October 15, 1845, before any act of the legislature had even occurred. For a brief time though, it changed the name back to Marthasville. The town name became official on December 26, 1845. The legislature amended the charter for the town of Marthasville to officially be called the town of Atlanta. The post office switched back again permanently in January 1846.

The naming of the town was settled. Additional amendments to the charter were needed to make Atlanta into something more than a stopover. The charter establishing the town of Marthasville was rudimentary and completely inadequate to the city's newfound prestige. The town commissioners established to govern Marthasville had already ceased to function.

However, not all the founders of Atlanta were in favor of establishing a more organized city government. It's easy to surmise from John Thrasher's initial experiences in Terminus that he might regard government organizations with some suspicion. He was the first person to move to the area in hopes of making his fortune from the plans for a railroad. These aspirations were ruined when the terminus changed locations. After settling back in the area, his feelings became quite clear when a group of citizens went to Milledgeville in 1846 with a proposal for the chartering of the new City of Atlanta. Thrasher recounted, "There was a charter procured, but a few of us declared that we would not have such laws as they had made. A lawyer said that he could break up the whole thing for $50 and we paid it and went on without a charter until the next meeting of the Legislature. This was in 1846."

Undaunted, the citizens of Atlanta supporting its charter for a new government continued. The town's schoolmaster, William N. White, wrote about much of the proceedings in his journal. As was most often the case, Jonathan Norcross was at the center of the work being done. The articles of incorporation of the City of Atlanta were then passed in the legislature and approved by Governor George W. Towns on December 29, 1847. Atlanta was now a city and would have a mayor, a city council, taxes and city ordinances.

While the charter for the incorporation of the city was still being written, Jonathan Norcross had the audacious idea to propose moving the capital of Georgia from Milledgeville to Atlanta. His first report to the committee on December 4, 1847, was met with laughter, but he had shown the usual foresight consistent with his impressive mind. The movement later gained support in Atlanta. Soon enough, his proposal would not seem so funny. The capital would remain in Milledgeville but moved to Atlanta in 1868.

The Macon and Western Railroad (formerly the Monroe Railroad) arrived into the newly renamed city of Atlanta from Macon on September 4, 1846. The celebration that accompanied its arrival was even bigger than the previous two railroad celebrations. Jonathan Norcross described the arrival of the Macon and Western to a reporter from the *Atlanta Constitution*:

> *This gave us our second railroad boom and it was tremendous, I can tell you. This was the time that the first railroad whistle was ever heard in*

The Whitehall Inn as it appeared in the 1840s and depicting the stagecoach driven by Tom Shivers. *Atlanta History Center.*

Atlanta. The engines on the Georgia and State roads were little fellows without any whistles. But the engine on the Macon road had a real whistle, and it made a great stir when it was first heard in Atlanta.

In the years since John Thrasher had laid out his little community of Deantown and the railroads had continued their march to connect at the point that had been laid out in the forest, the city had grown to around two thousand citizens. Farmers began bringing crops and livestock from many miles away to sell them in Atlanta's emerging markets. More trains began arriving. More people arrived. More businesses. More trouble.

22

Atlanta's First and Sometimes Forgotten Mayor and Council

Now that it had a charter, the next great milestone for the new City of Atlanta was to elect its first mayor and city council. This event would stir the city more than any thus far in the short history of Terminus, Marthasville and Atlanta. The day of the first election in Atlanta was January 29, 1848. It began with fights, and fights lasted through the day and into the night. The main rallying points for campaigning were in the city's drinking halls. It seemed every citizen was angry at some other citizen over some aspect of local politics, especially in Five Points.

The candidate chosen for the party that favored a more open and unregulated city was Moses Formwalt. Formwalt was a forthright, responsible man, but he was also "one of the boys." Every man who ran one of the forty or so drinking establishments, one for every fifty free adults in the city, knew young Moses. He was the tin and copper smith. He was the man who made the whiskey stills. His business that fronted the infamous Murrell's Row on Decatur Street was going well. Stills from Formwalt and his partner John E. Adams were being sold all over north Georgia, but Atlanta and its hard drinkers were the foundation of their success. This livelihood depended on the continued lackadaisical attitude of Atlanta toward drinking. The more drinkers there were in the city, the more drinking establishments, and the demand for stills would remain healthy.

Atlanta was somewhat unique in its political divisions. Unlike the rest of the South and the country overall where people were generally separated as Whigs or Democrats, Atlanta's election was a race between the Moral Party and the Free and Rowdy Party. Many commentators, including those at the time, described the race between the Moral Party and the Rowdies as a fight for law and order to triumph over chaos. That's an oversimplification of the real issues that were dividing the city. It's more accurate to say that it was a legitimate argument over increased governmental regulation of the city.

It's true that the gamblers, drunks and ruffians of the city were likely to vote for the Free and Rowdy candidates. It's not true that the Free and Rowdy Party was simply the party of the unruly. The Free and Rowdy Party did not exist simply to preserve and promote debauchery. It included many of the upright, leading citizens of the town, like John Thrasher and Benjamin Bomar, who served on the city council for many years and was instrumental in amending the Marthasville charter to create Atlanta.

Their platform didn't condone violence or serious crimes like muggings or the robbery of the train depots. Many were in favor of preserving the health of Atlanta's primary industries apart from the railroad, the industries supported by drinking and gambling. Many of the leaders of the Free and Rowdy Party were proprietors of these businesses. The Free and Rowdy Party also attracted those who mistrusted institutions and greater government influence. Many in the South, especially Georgians, mistrusted and opposed the federal government of the United States at this time.

Formwalt's opposition in the race to become Atlanta's first mayor had developed a well-known reputation since arriving a few years earlier. This was Jonathan Norcross, the Yankee reverend's son who owned the sawmill. His attitude was decidedly not in support of the continued growth of business surrounding drinking and debauchery. For the less sophisticated Atlantans who formed the voting base of the Free and Rowdy Party, Norcross was an overbearing, arrogant would-be dictator. The very name of the Moral Party implied superiority over the common people trying to get by. They would never allow the governing of the town to be turned over to the son of a Yankee reverend.

Atlanta pioneer David Mayer recalled, "In 1848 there were two hundred and fifteen votes polled at the election of Mayor. There was great excitement, and everybody drummed up." When the 215 votes were counted, the Rowdies won the day. Moses Formwalt became the first mayor of Atlanta. Other early Atlantans that we know were Rowdy supporters who filled positions in Formwalt's administration. Benjamin Bomar, who would become the city's second mayor, was on the city council. German Lester was made city marshal, and Tom Shivers, the stagecoach driver, became deputy city marshal.

A depiction of the polling place at Thomas Kile's Store on the day of the first election in Atlanta. *Atlanta History Center.*

Moses Formwalt did his best with what he had in his duties as mayor. What he had was not much though. The new city government was completely ineffective. Taxes were collected that year, but most people again refused to pay. The county gathered a total of $3,536.88, not enough to support many major city projects, even in 1848.

Years later, as the city grew, and the citizens of Atlanta made more noteworthy achievements, the name of Moses Formwalt was almost lost to Atlanta history. He served the city well and gave it his life. In 1852, he continued his city service in the role of deputy marshal. On May 1, 1852, while escorting a prisoner out of the mayor's council chambers, he was stabbed to death on the steps. He was only about thirty-one years old when he was murdered. He was then buried in Oakland Cemetery in an unmarked grave. For many years thereafter, Atlanta's first mayor and first officer to be killed in the line of duty was all but forgotten. And so it remained until 1916, when a committee was formed and a fitting monument was erected in Oakland Cemetery.

By far, the most common offense coming before the city council from 1848 to 1852 was disorderly conduct. This charge was used to capture a wide variety of the usual petty offenses occurring in the city every day like

Memorial in Oakland Cemetery for Moses Formwalt, Atlanta's first mayor, who was later murdered while serving as a Deputy Marshal. *Photo by the author.*

fighting, public drunkenness, rioting, firing your gun in the air, riding your horse in an unusual manner (we can only imagine what this meant), keeping a brothel open on Sunday and, of course, prostitution. The punishment was normally a fine of ten dollars or so.

The first and only time that Jonathan Norcross was brought before the city council occurred on April 3, 1848. He and Joshua Gilbert were each charged with disorderly conduct, probably a loud argument. Gilbert pleaded guilty and was fined ten dollars. Norcross, ever emphatic in asserting his moral stability, pleaded not guilty and was discharged.

Wandering livestock were also a problem. A free wandering group of cows broke into poor young nine-year-old George Gilman Smith's garden he had created behind McPherson's store and ate his crop. Billy Mann had also made a nuisance of himself by allowing his hogs to freely roam and find whatever food they could by wandering the Atlanta streets. A keg of ginger beer once spilled out in the street and was immediately quaffed up by the free-ranging hogs. Staggering, squealing, drunken hogs were then roaming the streets for the afternoon, creating a loud, hilarious spectacle. The city council then passed an ordinance prohibiting anyone from allowing their hogs to freely roam the streets.

At least one noteworthy but dubious accomplishment was made in 1848. The council constructed the city's first jail that year (most often called the calaboose) on the southwest corner of Alabama and Pryor Streets. The previous jail at Decatur had received limited use until the crime wave arrived from Atlanta. Decatur was glad to see Atlanta build its own jail and house its own criminals. However, instead of becoming a symbol of progress toward more civilization, the new Atlanta calaboose demonstrated the continued ridiculousness of its law enforcement.

The calaboose was constructed of hewn timbers three logs thick. The outside perimeter was about twelve feet square, about eight feet square on the inside. The door was secured by a wooden lock that was closed by a long brass key—about eight inches long and weighing a quarter of a pound. It must have looked formidable enough on the outside, but the jail had a hard-packed dirt floor. Prisoners were able to burrow out and under the walls, or if there were enough prisoners housed within or friends available to help without, they simply lifted the jail up on its side and the prisoners crawled out.

Not everything about 1848 Atlanta was dirt, drinking and violence. Like any place on a border of civilization, it was equally filled with the sloppy ingress of infrastructure and the raw persistence of the surrounding wilderness. While the streets ran with mud and spilled whiskey, the hills that still ran through the middle of town were filled with shading trees and bursting flowers. George Gilman Smith was one of few people who lived in Atlanta in 1848 possessing a poet's flair and a heart peaceful enough to stop and take notice of this passing magnificence:

> *I never saw more beauty than there was in the Springtime in the groves of Atlanta. All the undergrowth except the azaleas and dogwoods had lilies, trilliums, violets, pink roots, primroses—a fairer vision than any garden or exotic show now. Honeysuckles of every beautiful hue, deep red, pink, golden white, were in lavish luxuriance. The white dogwood was everywhere; the red woodbine and now and then a yellow jessamine climbed on the trees. When a stream was found it was clear and crystal. I have seen few things in the world so fair in this world of beauty, as were the Atlanta woods in 1848.*

23

THE END OF THE MEXICAN-AMERICAN WAR AND THE BEGINNING OF SOUTHERN SECESSION

O utside of city matters in the late 1840s, the attention of Atlantans and every American was focused on vast new western territories that had just been added to the country. The Mexican-American War ended in 1848, and its implications very nearly started the Civil War more than a decade before it began.

The United States would now be in possession of land that stretched from sea to shining sea. With the Treaty of Guadalupe that ended the war, U.S. territory suddenly expanded more than 525,000 square miles and included what would become Texas, Nevada, New Mexico, Utah, Arizona, California, Oklahoma, Kansas and parts of Colorado and Wyoming. This explosion of new territory meant that the trade coming out of the West was going to get much, much larger. The urgency for creating a railroad network to bring that trade east through the South increased. The political battle over how to incorporate these new territories into the United States far overshadowed any of the fighting on the battlefield.

More immediately and dramatically than the concern over western trade, the balance of power in Congress between slaveholding states and free states was being threatened. In 1820, the Missouri Compromise had postponed dealing with this issue by admitting Missouri as a slave state and Maine as a free state, thereby keeping the balance in Congress. As these new territories were added, national sentiment seemed to be shifting to freedom for all Americans. The South was increasingly threatened and infuriated.

The first proposals for the new territories were made before the Mexican-American War was even over. The Wilmot Proviso of 1846 proposed to Congress that all of the new territories would be free. Support for this notion became known as the Free Soil Movement, and its supporters were the Free Soilers. It passed the House of Representatives, where the northern states had a majority, but failed in the Senate.

Between 1846 and 1850, several proposals were made and failed, including allowing the new states to decide individually and extending the line of the Missouri Compromise (the 36°30′ parallel), to divide the southern slave states and free northern states all the way to the West Coast. In 1849, along with the gold rush, California requested to be admitted to the Union as a free state, threatening the balance once again and sending the North and South into more debate. Each time another proposal was debated and failed, the tensions and animosity between the North and the South grew. An increasing number of people in the South, including the powerful John C. Calhoun of South Carolina, began calling for secession from the Union. This was happening more than ten years before the start of the American Civil War. The leaders of this movement were dubbed the Fire-Eaters by northern legislators in reference to their radical platform.

The statements from the Southern Mechanics Convention of 1850 in Atlanta give a good illustration of how southerners were feeling intruded upon by the North. The convention as a body, want to "express, their firm and abiding devotion to the peculiar institution of the South as it is, and their utter and unqualified detestation of those Northern Abolitionists and Fanatics, who are constantly interfering with our interests and property."

The campaigning for support of the Fire-Eaters in the South brought the issue home to Atlanta in a handful of interesting incidents. Some of these gained national importance at the time.

24

The Brutal Stabbing of Representative Stephens by Senator Cone at the Atlanta Hotel

In the South, this debate over the disposition of the territory gained after the Mexican-American War became ugly and much more than political. It became a debate over what it meant to be a "true southerner and a true Georgian," something that was much more important to many southerners of the time than the policies of the Democrats or the Whigs. Atlanta took center stage in this and the western expansion debate in the fall of 1848. The incident involved a disagreement between two politicians in Atlanta, but it did more to add to Atlanta's reputation as a pit of violence than a place for intelligent, national debate.

On September 3, 1848, Representative Alexander Stephens took a train trip through Atlanta. The first speech Alexander Stephens ever made in his political career was in the Georgia House of Representatives to rally support for the building of railroads funded by the state. Now, he was a member of the U.S. House of Representatives from Georgia's Seventh District and enormously popular in Atlanta. He was a Unionist and had a friendly relationship with fellow Congressman Abraham Lincoln. Surprisingly though, he would later become the vice president of the Confederacy during the Civil War.

Representative Stephens was one of the invited speakers and honored guests coming to Atlanta to participate in a rally for the election of Zachary Taylor, the Whig presidential candidate in 1848. He was also in the midst of a feud with one of the Democrats in the Senate, Judge Francis Cone. The Clay Compromise was being debated as a possible solution to the disagreements over western expansion, the strongest that had been proposed thus far. As part of this proposal, Congress would sidestep the issue of slavery in the new western territories by leaving it to the citizens of the large Utah and New Mexico territories to decide. It was likely that most of the new states would choose against slavery. Apart from the shifting national sentiment toward greater equality, the climate of these new states was not conducive to the types of agriculture that the slave system supported. Cattle and sheep, instead of cotton and tobacco, were likely to be the most important products in the West.

The proposed compromise had mixed support from southern Whigs and was absolutely opposed by the southern Democrats. They tried to keep it from being put to a vote, but Stephens presented a motion and then voted to put the proposal on the table in the House of Representatives. This infuriated many of the southern Democrats, including Judge Francis Cone.

A rumor began to circulate that Judge Cone had said Stephens was "a damned little traitor to the South" for even considering the compromise. Stephens heard the rumor. He next saw Cone in person at a barbecue at the Glades in Putnam County and confronted him on the subject. Cone denied having said such a thing. Stephens replied that was quite good, because if he were to find out that it were true, he would slap Cone across the face. Cone took this as a joke at the time. The two men parted amiably. The remark must have needled at Cone's pride though. Three days later, he wrote Stephens a letter inquiring if the representative had been serious in the threat to slap him across the face if he had called Stephens a traitor.

At this point, some accounts of the story differ. Stephen responded to Cone in a letter. According to Cone and his supporters, he had not read the letter Stephens sent him when the two of them met again in Atlanta. According to other accounts, Cone had in fact gone to Atlanta looking to find Stephens and had tried to intercept him in Macon and Forsyth already.

Either way, Cone and Stephens met as Stephens walked up the steps of the Atlanta Hotel from the depot. He had arrived after supervising the unloading of his baggage from the train. The dinner bell had rung, and there were few people in the halls of the hotel at that time. Most had already gone to dinner.

Cone approached Stephens and asked if he had received the letter challenging him about the "I'll slap your jaws" comment. Stephens was a thin little wisp of a man but had never backed away from confrontation. He responded that he had received it and had sent the judge his response. Cone demanded to know what the response was. Stephens replied by saying, "You

View of the Atlanta Hotel in 1864 looking across the tracks just southwest of the depot and the State Square. *Library of Congress.*

have resorted to written correspondence and I have answered you in the same way. I shall make no verbal explanation touching the character of my written answer. That answer will speak for itself."

Cone then demanded a response once again, and Stephens refused to say what the letter had said once again. Cone replied that this second refusal could only mean that the letter did not contain anything like a retraction of Stephens's previous statement about slapping his face. Stephens replied, "You may assume what you please, but my written response shall speak for itself." Cone replied, "I then pronounce you a traitor to the South!"

As the words left Cone's mouth, Stephens brought up the whalebone walking stick he carried and whacked Cone across the face with it. In Cone's own words, "It caused an excitement to come over me which I am incapable of describing, and I immediately drew the knife from my pocket." He stabbed Stephens and once again demanded that Stephens retract his statement. Stephens answered by hitting Cone again with the walking stick. He then tried to twist the knife from Cone's hands. The judge was a big robust man of about two hundred pounds while Stephens is said to have only weighted about ninety pounds. The much larger judge flew into a bloody rage, throwing Stephens to the ground and brutally stabbing him five more times.

Four of the strikes cut into Stephens's right arm and hand as he tried to protect himself. Three of them entered his chest. One of the blows to his chest was severe and nearly took his life. The point of the knife Cone had used broke off on a rib and was lodged in Stephens's chest after the attack. The wounds to Stephens's right hand were deep and painful for a long time thereafter. His use of that hand was limited the rest of his life. In later photos of Stephens, his right arm is always held forward a bit awkwardly with his index finger held outstretched. This is probably due to the stiffness from the injuries he suffered in Atlanta.

The landlord of the hotel and a man named Terrence Doonan ran to the scene and dragged Cone off Stephens. If they hadn't, the representative probably would have been murdered. Confusion and panic swept into the hotel and the State Square over the next few minutes. The deputy marshal, Tom Shivers appeared on the scene but did little to calm and organize the crowd. He probably added to the confusion when he fired his gun in the air several times. He was also later accused of assaulting some of those present. He also failed to detain or apprehend Cone as the judge slipped away from the scene. Stephens was treated by a doctor with tourniquets while he lay bleeding. He was then carefully carried to the home of John Mims, the agent of the Georgia Railroad.

When he was able to be moved, Stephens was brought back to the Atlanta hotel and stayed there for several days under a doctor's care. He was evidently a tough little man. When it came time for the rally in Atlanta eleven days later on September 14, he refused to be absent, although he was still badly injured. He rallied out of bed and called for his carriage to bring him to Walton Spring. When he emerged from the hotel, he was met by a mass of supporters. In a show of respect and affection, they unhitched the horses from his carriage and drew it from the hotel to the spring themselves. G.G. Smith was present to see this short journey from the hotel: "I remember the pale face of the little man as he sat in the carriage."

The rally was a huge success. It drew listeners from more than fifty miles around Atlanta. The first American flag that ever flew in Atlanta was drawn out and unfurled over the offices of the *Intelligencer* newspaper by Cornelius Hanleiter to honor the proceedings.

Stephens was the star of the rally but stayed in a chair for most of the event. Robert Toombs acted as a replacement for Alexander Stephens. When it seemed like Stephens's turn had come to speak, the crowd demanded a speech, but he was unable to do so. He rose and greeted them but apologized that a speech would be hazardous to his health. He gave only a brief story about a veteran he had heard of returning from war to New Orleans after a long march through the far West under General Wool.

Portrait of Alexander Stephens. The awkward position of his fingers in all later photos is probably due to injuries he received when stabbed in Atlanta. *Library of Congress.*

The man was cared for and then asked if there was anything else with which the citizens could provide him. The man replied, "No. Nothing at all." As he walked away though, the man thought better of it. He returned and said, "I have *one more* request to make and but one; and that is do not forget to vote and be sure to vote for General Taylor!" General Zachary Taylor, the Whig candidate, had gained national popularity for his service in the recent Mexican-American War.

In the days that followed the stabbing, Judge Cone published an open letter describing his version of the incident. Instead of vindicating him, many felt the letter proved that the Judge had arrived in Atlanta with the intention of confronting Stephens armed with his knife. In the letter, he admits that he discussed how to respond to Stephens's comment about slapping him with friends. "It was thought best and agreed that I should call upon Mr. Stephens, and ask of him whether he had seriously threatened to slap my face." He then goes on to say that he found Stephens in Forsyth and decided it was not the right place to confront him. He then went to Atlanta, where he confronted Stephens. The judge provides no other explanation for going to Atlanta other than this confrontation. Then, as the judge began to pronounce Stephens a traitor, he was struck in the face and describes how he drew the knife while flying into a blind rage.

Stephens tried to continue on the campaign trail for Taylor, but he later had to withdraw because of the continued pain in his hand. Over the next few weeks, Judge Cone was banned from speaking at future political engagements when Alexander Stephens was also on the bill. Stephens's hand never fully healed, and he had trouble straightening some of his fingers, as can be seen here.

A true bill was found against Judge Cone by the DeKalb Grand Jury for the September term of 1848. This was the same jury that would indict William Terrell for the murder of James McWilliams. Judge Cone was arraigned and pleaded guilty to the charge. Amazingly, Cone was released with only a fine of $800 by Judge E.Y. Hill.

Despite the enthusiasm and rhetoric for the Whigs generated by Stephens and others, and the fact that Taylor carried Georgia and the election, the Democrats won in DeKalb County that year. Unfortunately, Taylor did not serve as a president for even a full term. He died of a stomach flu on July 9, 1850. All businesses in Atlanta were closed in a day of mourning.

25

Tom Shivers, Atlanta's Rogue Deputy Marshal

One of the participants in the incident that nearly killed Alexander Stephens was Tom Shivers, Atlanta's deputy marshal in 1848. Atlanta was often compared to a frontier town of the Wild West during the 1840s. If that is so, then its most brutish citizen with the dangerous spirit of a gunslinger was probably Tom Shivers. Although he was elected to be deputy marshal and later reelected, no other citizen appeared before the city council for public offenses as many times as Tom Shivers did. Most of these charges were dismissed during 1848, but his notorious actions continued to accumulate.

As the stagecoach driver on its route between Decatur and Marietta, Shivers was well known to most of the town long before he became deputy marshal. In fact, he was one of the first people to become familiar with the area that would become Atlanta even before such pioneers as John Thrasher and Sarah Carlisle. When he settled in the new city of Atlanta and was elected deputy marshal by the new city council, he was twenty-nine years old. He was married to a woman named Eliza (twenty-seven) and had two young children. His family responsibilities do not seem to have curtailed any of his exertions into danger, both lawful and unlawful.

The first of more than a dozen times Shivers was charged and appeared before the city council was on July 17, 1848. Several citizens were accused of gambling, and James Buford was accused of keeping a gaming house. All the men were discharged, but Deputy Marshal Shivers was also charged with having been overly rough with the accused citizens. "The case of Shivers was taken up and on examination it appeared that what he did was to keep peace ordered that he be discharged." We can only imagine that perhaps Shivers had to hit someone in the head to get them under control or something of that sort. He was reluctantly judged to have acted within his duties, but his rough methods escalated from there.

The second time Shivers was called before the council was for his conduct surrounding the incident where Judge Francis Cone nearly murdered Representative Alexander Stephens at the Atlanta Hotel by stabbing him repeatedly with a knife. Shivers was charged with several offenses on this occasion, including "refusing to do his duty," "shooting," "aiding in shooting in the street," "refusing to suppress a row," "disorderly conduct in the street" and for an assault on Eldridge Morgan. The charges were dismissed except for Shivers's failure to act and the assault on Morgan. These were both held over for a future meeting. Shivers failed to appear at the next meeting and was fined two dollars. Despite his absence and failure to respond to the charges, both cases were eventually dismissed.

Toward the end of 1848, upon requesting a report from both the marshal and the deputy marshal in November, the council deemed Shivers's report unsatisfactory. Benjamin Bomar, who would become Atlanta's second mayor, was particularly frustrated with Shivers. He was most often the member of city council demanding an explanation of Shivers's actions as deputy marshal or lack thereof. During the same meeting in October 1848, Alderman Bomar called for the marshal and deputy marshal to report on the moneys they had received for the treasury.

The charge of an unsatisfactory report and request for an accounting of money collected by the deputy marshal may sound like simple city bureaucracy, but it was more serious. One of the primary duties of the deputy marshal was to collect fines; these would then be reported and handed over to the city council as municipal revenue. These collections could involve thousands of dollars. It seems like a reasonable conclusion that the council suspected Tom Shivers was collecting fines and pocketing the money.

The city council finally made a clear statement about Shivers's performance as a deputy marshal near the end of his one-year term. The customary resolution was passed to pay the deputy marshal his wages on November 13, 1848, but with the same stroke Shivers was tried for another offense of disorderly conduct. The record doesn't indicate what Shivers did to earn this latest charge. Whatever it was, this time, they found him guilty and fined him twenty-five dollars and dismissed him from his services to the city.

In 1848, the deputy marshal position probably did not receive an annual salary more than $150. A fine of $25 was a large and serious one for disorderly conduct at that time and a fair share of his overall wages. E.T. Hunnicutt was then appointed deputy marshal on December 28, 1848. The position of deputy marshal was eliminated in 1849.

Tom Shivers was far from finished imposing his own view of justice on the new city of Atlanta. He was just getting started. A few years after being dismissed as deputy marshal, he participated in the declaration of a new set of laws in Atlanta in direct, open defiance to the city government and later in the only bona fide quick-draw showdown in the streets of Atlanta.

26

The Killing of James McWilliams by William Terrell

September 1848 was a bloody month for the new city of Atlanta. While Alexander Stephens was still in town convalescing in the Atlanta Hotel, Atlanta had its first cold-blooded murder. It occurred once again over Whig versus Democrat politics and was connected to the issue of western expansion.

Though crime for personal gain was rampant in Atlanta, it does not seem to have been the root cause for most of its violence. Politics were growing increasingly passionate, and political arguments were at the root of most of the bloodshed that occurred. Atlantans were passionate about politics, most often debated in the barrooms and largely fueled by alcohol.

George Featherstonhaugh gave a colorful description of the political discourse during the mid-1800s during a trip he took through the Georgia mountains:

> *What these parsnip-looking country fellows seem to enjoy most is political disputation in the barroom of their filthy taverns, exhibiting much bitterness against each other in supporting their respective candidates of the Union and State-rights parties which divide the State, and this without seeming to have the slightest information respecting the principles of either. Execration and vociferation, and "Well, I'm for [_____], by _____!" were the nearest approach to logic ever made in my presence.*

The incident happened in Atlanta, but both the perpetrator of this murder, William Terrell, and his unfortunate victim, James McWilliams, were from nearby Panthersville. Both were also from noteworthy, well-respected families of the county. There was a simmering feud between the two families that went back to the Revolutionary War. Both of the men's grandfathers had fought for America at the Battle of Camden in 1780 but under differing commanding officers. One fought under General Horatio Gates and the other under the heroic Frenchman, General Baron Johann DeKalb, the namesake for DeKalb County. The Terrells felt the McWilliams were not true patriots and had only reluctantly supported the revolution.

This dislike between Terrell and McWilliams was intensified by the coming election. McWilliams was a Whig like Alexander Stephens and their candidate Zachary Taylor. Terrell was a Democrat like Judge Francis Cone and their candidate Senator Lewis Cass. Terrell and McWilliams had met many times before, and their mutual dislike was well known. They first saw each other on that fateful day at the rally at Walton Spring where Alexander Stephens had stood with his injuries and said a few words.

The barbecue was an enormous event and well attended. G.G. Smith was there: "I recall little save about the great barbecue, where whole hogs and oxen were roasted, and the viands were spread on long tables, and the wild rush of the hungry crowd to snatch the smoking food. I remember the torchlight procession and the transparencies and the great crowds of strainers."

As had probably happened most times they met, Terrell and McWilliams exchanged harsh words when they saw each other. That night, after the rally was over, most of Atlanta and the droves of people visiting from the nearby country were carousing on Decatur Street. Amid the crowds, the two men crossed paths for the second time that day, much to their mutual regret.

About 8:30 p.m., Terrell was walking down Decatur Street with his friend William Henson and loudly proclaiming the superiority of his candidate, Cass, probably after enjoying much refreshment at the rally. Behind him, McWilliams and his brother David were on horseback and loudly proclaiming the superiority of their candidate, Taylor. Terrell and his friend Henson stopped at Kile's General Store to buy some of the beloved ginger cakes sold there.

Once McWilliams and his brother caught up to them, the four men began a loutish squabble from opposite sides of Decatur Street. The shouting

A view looking northwest on Decatur Street in 1864. This is the spot where McWilliams was murdered by William Terrell. *Library of Congress.*

and insults escalated. Terrell called McWilliams "a Tory and a coward," a reference back to the animosity that began with each of their grandfathers during the Revolution.

McWilliams had heard enough. He dismounted from his horse and walked to the middle of the street, challenging Terrell to do the same. Terrell obliged. They met and began exchanging punches. They then grasped each other and fell to the street. Like Alexander Stephens, Terrell was a small man but feisty. McWilliams was a larger man and got the better of Terrell. Holding Terrell on the ground, McWilliams was about to finish the fight when Terrell then produced a six-inch white-handled knife and sank it into McWilliams's left side.

McWilliams grunted, and the fight was over. He fell, bleeding badly into the dirt of Decatur Street. Terrell and his friend fled the scene immediately after the stabbing and spent the night lying under cover in a nearby field.

A PROCLAMATION.

Georgia.

BY GEORGE W. TOWNS,

Governor of said State.

WHEREAS, this department has been officially informed that William Terrell committed the offence of murder on the body of James McWilliams in the county of DeKalb on the 14th September instant, and that the said Terrell has fled from justice.

I have therefore though: proper to issue this my Proclamation, hereby offering a reward of *one hundred and fifty dollars* for the apprehension and delivery of the said Wm. Terrell to the Sheriff of DeKalb county in said State.

And I do moreover charge and require all officers. *Civil* and *Military*. in this State. to be vigilant in endeavoring to apprehend the said William Terrell, in order that he may be brought to trial for the offence with which he stands charged.

Given under my hand and the Great Seal of the State. at the Capitol in Milledgeville, this twenty-eighth day of September. eighteen hundred and forty-eight, and of the independence of the United States, the seventy-third.

GEO. W. TOWNS.

By the Governor.

N. C. BARNETT, Sec'y. of State.

DESCRIPTION:

Said Terrell is a small man, about nineteen years of age; blue eyes, and very cross-eyed; light or rather sandy hair; about five feet, seven or eight inches-high; weighs about one hundred and twenty pounds; slim or light and spare built.

The manhunt for William Terrell describes him as a man of about 120 pounds and "very cross-eyed." *The Federal Union, October 10, 1848.*

McWilliams was carried into the Kile house, and his wounds were dressed. Unlike Alexander Stephens, who had suffered such a similar injury only a couple hundred yards away less than two weeks earlier, McWilliams did not survive the wound in his side. Not long after McWilliams was laid out in the Kile house, Dr. Joshua Gilbert declared he would not survive. James McWilliams died at 2:00 p.m. the next day.

Terrell then went out on the run for several months. A manhunt was initiated across the South to find him. The description of Terrell sent out to aid his capture said he was "a small man, about nineteen years of age; blue eyes and very cross-eyed; light or rather sandy hair; about five feet seven or eight inches high; weighs about one hundred twenty pounds; slim or light and spare built."

He was arrested in Alabama and hauled back to Decatur. Terrell was found guilty of voluntary manslaughter in March 1850 and sentenced to four years of hard labor at the penitentiary in Milledgeville by Judge E.Y. Hill, the same judge who had sentenced Judge Francis Cone to only a fine. For a brief time, it seemed Terrell might be given a mistrial over the misspelling of a juror's name. A request for a new trial went to the state supreme court and was denied. Terrell served out all four years of his sentence in Milledgeville. Perhaps a little ironically, this meant he was still virtually employed in the city of Atlanta. The penitentiary was the main producer of railroad cars that were sent back down the rails to Atlanta.

27

THE SLAVE DEPOT AND
THE MOB FROM MACON

In January 1850, the issue of western expansion looked as if it would be settled. Henry Clay, a Whig from Kentucky and a giant of the Senate who has often been called the "Great Compromiser," proposed a compromise to end the debates on western expansion (usually called the Clay Compromise). The initial proposal was a package of five different resolutions closely tied to the issue of expansion. These were that (1) the northern border of Texas would be set as the 36°30′ parallel; (2) California would join the union as a new, free state; (3) the citizens of the large Utah and New Mexico Territories would decide for themselves whether slavery would be legal within their borders; (4) the slave trade would be banned within the District of Columbia; and (5) a new, strengthened Fugitive Slave Law would be enacted, strictly requiring law enforcement in free states to capture and return any slaves who escaped from slave states.

The most famous debate in the history of the Senate ensued over the next several months, led by the Fire-Eater senator John C. Calhoun and the Free-Soiler senator Daniel Webster over Clay's proposals. It was the last debate among these three senators, whom many historians consider some of the most important in American history.

The Fire-Eaters were not at all pleased with the compromise. In the time they had before its impending passage, John C. Calhoun and the other Fire-Eater senators like Robert Barnwell Rhett of South Carolina, worked feverishly to get support for the secession of southern states from the Union.

In the end, the compromise blunted the overall southern appetite for civil war enough to get general support from Clay's fellow Whigs. As one of his final acts in Congress, Henry Clay convinced Senator Stephen Douglas of Illinois to take up the Clay Compromise and propose it as five separate bills in the Senate. This strategy succeeded, and the compromise was passed in September 1850. The Great Compromiser lived up to his reputation. The Civil War was temporarily averted.

Amid the Fire-Eaters' campaigning and frustration over the Clay Compromise, one of Atlanta's first publishers made his opinion on the matter widely known and sparked a strong, public reaction he probably didn't expect. This was Cornelius Hanleiter, another of the city's leading citizens in the late 1840s. Hanleiter learned the printing trade after starting as an apprentice at age eleven. He then brought this trade to Atlanta after passing through Augusta, Macon, Forsyth and then Madison, where he published the *Southern Miscellany*. He moved the operations of the *Miscellany* to Atlanta in 1847.

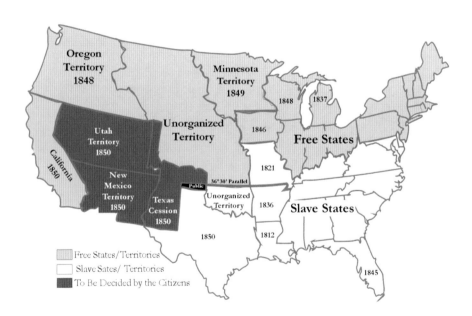

The United States as it existed in 1850 after the Clay Compromise. *Sketch by the author using sources from Library of Congress.*

Telegraph lines arrived to Atlanta in May 1849. It was an extension of the Macon and Western Railroad company, the Macon and Western Branch Telegraph Company. In 1849, Hanleiter withdrew from the publishing business to become the town's first telegraph operator. Hanleiter's decision may have been driven by a desire for more stable employment, as he was preparing to remarry. He and his second wife, Ann Elizabeth Shaw, married in September 1850. Hanleiter's first wife, Mary Ann Ford, passed away in 1848. His son William and another boy named Andrew Shaw were Atlanta's first telegraph messengers. The first message sent from Atlanta by telegraph was to an executive of the Macon and Western Railroad.

The operations of the *Southern Miscellany* were sold to a consortium of other Atlanta pioneers, including Jonathan Norcross, Ira McDaniel, Benjamin Bomar and Zachariah Rice. These gentlemen changed the name of the *Southern Miscellany* to the *Weekly Atlanta Intelligencer* and brought out the first issue on June 1, 1849. The *Intelligencer* became a loud voice in support of the Moral Party and its candidate for the fourth mayor of Atlanta, Jonathan Norcross.

A month before his wedding, in August 1850, Hanleiter was continuing to keep his hand in the newspaper business by writing frequent letters to the editor of the *Georgia Citizen* in Macon highlighting the top news events in

The office of the *Atlanta Intelligencer* just south of the tracks and west of the State Square. *Library of Congress.*

Atlanta. He wrote under the alias "Gabriel" and often expressed his opinions about what was happening in the young city. His alias was dramatically revealed in 1850.

The debate over western expansion was the top headline across the country. In the South, the debate was volatile. It had progressed into a union versus disunion debate, and Georgians were divided. Most Georgians were still in favor of remaining in the Union, but the passion in the disagreement was growing. The issue of slavery was not open for debate in Georgia, at least publicly. In the public forum, an accusation that a person was not fully supportive of slavery got a reaction similar to being accused of being a witch in the 1700s. The accused would immediately deny the accusation but normally find themselves publicly ridiculed and ostracized nevertheless.

Along with the warehouses, railroad buildings, stores, mills and numerous bars, a building called the Holland House was being added to downtown Atlanta for the purpose of buying and selling slaves. On August 22, 1850, Hanleiter wrote a fascinating letter expressing his opinion of this new depot that was then published in the *Georgia Citizen*:

> *Among the numerous buildings that are now in the process of erection in this city, is one of brick, in full view of and scarcely a stone's throw from the Atlanta Hotel, which is designated as a depot for the safe keeping and sale of negroes. Two-thirds of our people, who know the purpose for which it is intended, are opposed to its completion, but, as yet, I have heard of no steps being taken to prevent it. On sabbath last however, the heavy rain with which we were visited washed away nearly one-third of the eastern wall—thus showing (to the minds of omen believers at least) that Providence disapproves of the unhallowed purpose for which the building is designed. For my own part I am free to say I should rejoice to see it razed to the ground as often as its owner rebuilds it.*
>
> *The Hon. R.B. Rhett passed down on this morning's train to attend the Disunion Mass Meeting to be held in your city on Thursday next. I remember to have seen one valiant South Carolinian "take the back door" of your Courthouse in 1840, for giving utterance to objectionable sentiments; and I trust that your citizens are still too much attached to the constitution and laws of their glorious country to permit Mr. Rhett or any other "foreigner" to desecrate either now, with impunity. A coat of tar and feathers would be a suitable covering for all such mad-caps during the present excitement.*
>
> *...yours truly, Gabriel*

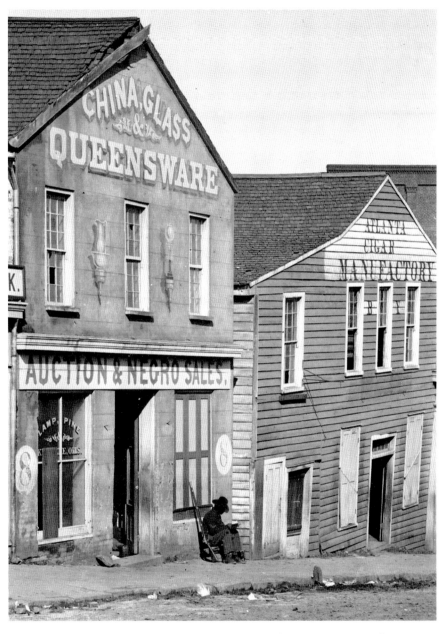

The slave depot (shown in 1864) was just across the street from the *Intelligencer* offices on the south side of the tracks. *Library of Congress*.

Even though it concerns a separate topic from the slave depot, Hanleiter probably included the second paragraph purposefully with the first. The building of the depot coincided with a mass meeting on the topic of the western expansion and slavery in the West. Hanleiter expresses clear disapproval of the slave depot being built in Atlanta. He then says one of the main leaders of the movement to include slavery in the new western territories, Robert Rhett, should be tarred and feathered.

It's difficult to make a firm conclusion. Hanleiter later denied the letter was meant to express disapproval of slavery, and he would go on to be a Confederate colonel during the Civil War. Nevertheless, this letter appears to be a clear condemnation of slavery. He also published it the day of a mass meeting in Macon, where the paper was published. It doesn't seem likely that was a coincidence. Hanleiter may have been trying to spark debate over the institution of slavery in general. If so, he woefully underestimated the fury of the opposition and the southern appetite for slavery debate.

After the letter was published on the morning of August 29, 1850, it became a central topic of discussion that day all over Macon. Before the mass meeting even started, there were calls to run Andrews, the editor, out of town and force him to reveal Gabriel's true name. There were even ominous mentions that the "hanging process" should begin. Andrews delivered an explanation for how he had come to publish the article, saying it had been set into the type by his son and he had never actually read it, though he doubted he would have taken it out. This explanation was never read during the mass meeting though.

When they met, the disunionists agreed to declare their official and public condemnation of the *Georgia Citizen* and its editor. A committee of fifteen was elected to deliver the judgment of the association to the editor of the newspaper. Outside the newspaper offices, they put up a placard demanding that the publisher, Andrews, never publish his paper again in Macon and that he divulge the name of the writer from Atlanta. If he did not do so, the citizens of Macon would "compel his precipitated departure." He would be run out of town—probably on a rail or tarred and feathered.

The committee of fifteen grew to a mob in Macon that night. They set up a vigil outside the offices of the *Georgia Citizen*, daring Andrews to publish his paper. Andrews was forced to close for a day and published only a half sheet the following day, lacking the time for a full edition.

On the first point, he refused. In the half sheet, Andrews rejected the demands that he stop publishing and said he was ready to respond in kind for any violence the mob might choose to bring to him. He also vehemently swore to his deep southern roots and support of the institution of slavery. To the mob's second demand that he reveal the true name of "Gabriel," Andrews caved to the pressure and revealed the name of Hanleiter to the mob.

In his review of the event, Andrews suggested there were several less political reasons for the reaction of the mob. The members of the Southern Rights Association had a meeting the previous Thursday, which, according to Andrews, "doubtless kindled anew all the fire of their souls against their opposing brethren." They were incensed and mortified too, at the "failure of their hopes and expectations" in that attendance of the mass meeting was much poorer than they had hoped. Andrews also reported that among the members of the mob was a man named James Dean; he owned the slave depot in question and was incensed at the threat to his business more than his political beliefs. There were also several people who were on staff with the *Macon Telegraph*, the principal competition for the *Georgia Citizen*. The *Telegraph* was in ardent support of the Democrats while the *Citizen* supported the Whigs.

Now, armed with name Hanleiter, some of the mob went looking for him. Upon passing back home to or through Atlanta on the train, several of them tried to incite more outrage and action among Atlantans. They succeeded. Another mass disunion meeting was held on September 14, and it was attended by around three hundred people in Atlanta. In this meeting, they crafted and then circulated a letter expressing their "decided condemnation of the striking assimilation to abolitionism which its [the letter's] sentiments manifest." A letter of complaint was delivered to Mayor Wyllys Buell demanding that Hanleiter should be expelled from the state of Georgia. As a decent, reasonable man, Buell took no action. However, Hanleiter's new employers, the Western Branch Telegraph Company, acquiesced. Hanleiter was dismissed from his position just a few months after he had sold his business and taken the new position and a couple of weeks before he was to remarry.

This story of Hanleiter and the mob from Macon doesn't just portray an interesting piece of history about Atlanta in 1850 and serve up some important insights into the mood of the entire state at that time. This incident is also connected and foreshadows other important events that happened in Atlanta over the following months. Tensions were rising largely because of the debate over slavery. Most southerners felt the battle lines were now clearly drawn between themselves and the northern states bent on abolition or, as they viewed it, destruction of the traditional southern institutions.

This author believes Hanleiter, and perhaps Andrews as well, misjudged the general feelings of other Georgians. They misjudged the degree to which other Georgians were already feeling angry and ready to fight over the issue of slavery and the progress of the abolitionist agenda.

All of this contributed to the inevitability of a showdown in Atlanta. The supporters of both the Moral Party and the Rowdy Party were still growing and becoming increasingly bold in expressing their views on the city. The mainstream city to come would have to confront the unruly city that it was.

28

BEING BLACK IN 1850 ATLANTA

T his book has been dedicated "To the people who built the Georgia railroads with their hands and did more than anyone else to create a great new city in the South but received very little of the reward or the recognition for having done it." That dedication refers in part to immigrants and Native Americans but much more to the enslaved Black Georgians who were employed or owned by the railroads that led to the creation of the city of Atlanta.

The Black experience in the South of the mid-1800s is obviously a story of oppression. In Atlanta of the late 1840s and early 1850s, another more uplifting side to that story was unfolding. Looking closely, one can see the mostly hidden but rising tide that would bring about the end of slavery in America. The country was changing. In the South, Atlanta was at the forefront of this change.

On a relative basis, the role of Black Americans in Atlanta was becoming more progressive than in the rest of the South. It was a new city with evolving attitudes. Many of Atlanta's city leaders, including two of its first four mayors, came from places where there were more progressive attitudes toward the role of Black Americans in society. Wyllys Buell was from Connecticut, and Jonathan Norcross was from Maine.

The role of Black people in Atlanta was much more closely intertwined with white residents than in rural settings. Though it depended on agriculture for most of the products transported by the railroads, Atlanta's economy was not agriculturally based. Everything in Atlanta depended on the railroads, and Black people had a closer role in keeping the railroads operating than in agriculture.

Many of the Black people in Atlanta had greater choice over their own daily activities than African Americans elsewhere. As farmers had done when the railroads were being built, many of the enslaved people in Atlanta were hired out for work from nearby farms. When the prices for cotton and other products were low, these farmers could earn more by getting a wage for their slaves. Once employed in the city, these slaves would often live away from their owners for long periods of time and act under their own recognizance for most of their days.

The Black population of 1850 made up about 20 percent of the city's population. There were 493 Black slaves (216 men and 277 women) and 19 free Black people living in Atlanta (6 men and 13 women). The total population of the city was 2,572. The Black proportion of the city grew rapidly in later years. By 1870, Black Americans made up nearly half of the city's population.

In most southern cities, there were far more enslaved women than men. That's because most of the slaves working in cities were performing domestic household tasks for wealthier white families instead of agricultural work. Female slaves were also often forced to work in prostitution in many cities. This may have happened in Atlanta, where there was a lot of prostitution, but it's unclear and there is no direct evidence of it. Male slaves were given skilled work to perform that they often did alongside other free Black and white laborers like blacksmithing or carpentry.

Most of the resident slaves in Atlanta lived in the more affluent neighborhoods. Willis and Sarah Carlisle, two of the first to arrive in Terminus, had a slave living in their house named Rebecca Sweat. John and Mary Mims, the agent for the Georgia Railroad and his wife, had a slave living in their house named Rubara Smith. One slave, Rhoda Moss, and her three children, York, Georgia and Eliza, lived together in the home of Barney Riley, an Irish former railroad worker. Riley is unlikely to have been a wealthy man. It's possible that Rhoda Moss lived with him as his wife, not his slave.

Nearly all of the free Black women in Atlanta were employed in the washing and ironing trade. At least one of them, Mary Leach, was also employed as a prostitute. A few others reported no particular occupation. Most of the free Black men were employed as common laborers.

There was at least one independent family of free Black people living in Atlanta in 1850. This was Milly and Walker Ruff. Walker was a blacksmith,

Two Atlanta residents washing and ironing, virtually the only legitimate job open to women in antebellum Atlanta. *Atlanta History Center.*

and Milly added to the family funds doing washing and ironing. They made enough in this occupation to have their own home in the Snake Nation district. Mary Roach came with Milly from Warrenton, Georgia, and lived with them in Atlanta. Like Milly, she was a washer and ironer.

Another well-employed free Black person in 1851 Atlanta was Reubin Norman, a barber. He was probably formerly enslaved by Henry and Mary Latimer. At the time of the 1850 census, though already free, he lived with the Latimers as well as five other Black Atlantans. He prospered well enough as a free barber that he was still doing it nearly ten years later in 1860. This is significant. The barbershop of the 1800s was an important place for city residents to meet and exchange the news. Norman's shop must have served white clients, and this would have given him a very special status among the Black residents. He would have had access to information overheard in his shop and relationships with white Atlantans that other Black residents would never have had. This added status to the local barber and barbershops as a place to exchange local news and interact with other residents is a large part of what led Black-owned barbershops to become central cornerstones of Black communities, especially after the Civil War. Reubin Norman could be regarded as a father of this institution in Atlanta.

Though he didn't reside in Atlanta, there was another free Black man in the area worthy of note and remembering. His name was Newton Lowry. It's not clear if he owned some land or was a tenant to another landowner. However, he was the first Black farmer making a go of it in Dekalb County. In 1851, when he registered with the county to receive his certificate showing proof of his freedom, he was just fourteen years old.

Though many Atlantans were more open to seeing Black Georgians in new roles, the general attitude of white Georgians toward slaves in the late 1840s and early 1850s betrays a feeling of enormous fear. The population of slaves in many counties approached or even surpassed that of white residents. White people were terrified of any organization slaves might make to inspire one another or organize resistance. This was made clear in the reaction to the book about the outlaw John Murrell that described a plan for a widespread slave insurrection. The story was almost certainly a complete fabrication, but the panic it caused led to several deaths for supposed accomplices in the plot.

The same kind of panicky suspicion took place in Atlanta in 1851 concerning a widely known slave named Henry Long. Long's case gained national attention because it was one of the first applications of the strengthened Fugitive Slave Law passed as part of the Clay Compromise of 1850. In the fall of 1850, Long was discovered in New York working as a free man and a waiter at the Pacific Restaurant. He had been working there for nearly two years when it was discovered that he was, in fact, a fugitive from Virginia enslaved by John T. Smith of Russell County, Virginia. The claim was briefly fought in the New York courts, but in the end, Smith's claims prevailed in the District Court and Long was forced to return to bondage in Virginia.

Smith believed his slave had been "ruined" by his exposure to people who didn't treat him as property in New York. It was thought Long would not be of use in his previous duties. After Long was extradited to the South, Smith sold him to a slave trader named Clopton in Richmond for $750. Clopton then brought Long to Atlanta and sold him through its infamous slave depot. Long was purchased in Atlanta by Captain Lloyd, the owner of the Washington Hall Hotel, who took advantage of the skills Long had acquired in the North. He made Long his head waiter at the hotel. The Atlanta Hotel and Washington Hall hotels were both opened in 1846.

Long lived in better physical conditions than most slaves under these circumstances but never as anything other than a slave. It seems Captain Lloyd may have been enlightened enough to treat Long with some respect, but certainly not all of those who ate in his restaurant felt the same way. Long was constantly watched with suspicion. Some even thought he had been sent to Atlanta by the Free Soilers of the North with a secret mission to inspire southern slaves to resistance. In the summer of 1851, Long was observed meeting with other Black Atlantans outside the hotel in the evening. Some of the people who witnessed him doing this were alarmed and reported it to the hotel and the marshal. John and several other slaves were arrested and brought before the mayor on July 29, 1851. The names of the others arrested were reported as Peter, Huff, Henry Humphreys, Burrell, Stephen Cammack, John Bostwick, Sandy, Levi and Jim. Some were employed by the hotel, including the cook. Others were from businesses nearby. The men were whipped and charged with stealing from the hotel and organizing a "colored society" to inspire slave insurrection.

In the end, Long and the others who were arrested were found innocent. The meetings they had been holding were to gamble together, not to plan an uprising. They were questioned by the mayor and council and then released.

Slavery became a fiercely protected institution of the South because it supported the large plantation-style agricultural economy and later became a piece of southern identity when it was felt other states were trying to remove it. By the late 1830s, this system was already breaking down. It remained strong in some areas, particularly in the middle interior of Georgia. The overall strength of southern agriculture was waning, though. The newer western states, like Arkansas, Missouri, Wisconsin and Iowa, were now producing most of the country's agricultural commerce. In the places touched by the railroad, it became more useful to use slaves to build the railroads than to farm. Unknowingly and unintentionally, Georgia southerners had given their enslaved population exposure to new, more technology-focused jobs. As the railroads continued to employ slaves, many Black Georgians were gaining skills that white southerners lacked. Once employed by the railroads, slaves progressed into more skilled labor like blacksmithing, ironwork, carpentry and mechanics.

As the country expanded farther west in 1850, slavery was becoming less important to the overall economy. Most of this new land was flat and arid. It was more suited to ranching than big plantation-style farming. The balance was shifting toward states that opposed slavery or at least didn't view the practice with the same importance.

The resolutions of the Southern Mechanics Convention that took place in Atlanta in 1851 very clearly illustrated the struggle between emerging new opportunities for Black southerners brought by the railroads and the attempts of white society to suppress them. The first complaint of the association was that the penitentiaries were being used for much of the mechanical work now available in the state. The penitentiary at Milledgeville was the primary manufacturer of the state's railroad cars. The association felt that "the importance of these jobs must be raised to a lofty profession. Mechanical arts in Georgia are viewed as base and disgraceful. This is entirely wrong."

The same view held true for teaching slaves to perform mechanical work. The criminal motives underlying slavery are very clearly articulated in the association's resolutions on this point:

> *Mechanical pursuits elevate the Negro's mind and quicken his intellect, leading to a desire to read and write, the gratification of which is often obtained in a clandestine manner, by which he is furnished with facilities for making money, and led into depravity and dissipation, thereby making him restless and unhappy, and an unsafe associate for the dutiful and contented negroes of the State.*

Despite the constant effort to protect it in the South and the dependence on the South to provide cotton for northern mills, the end of slavery was approaching. Everyone knew it except perhaps the Fire-Eaters and their followers. Black slaves in Atlanta were being more exposed to how people lived in other places, more equally with whites. It would be impossible to suppress a large population of Americans once they had a better sense of the great potential they had in their country.

Permeating the tension was a vague generalized feeling that the South had lost when the Clay Compromise was passed. The North had succeeded in its overall goal, which was to apply increasing pressure that would eventually break down slavery. It was becoming apparent that the end of slavery was now a question of "when," not "if." White southerners felt increasingly demoralized and persecuted. They would soon react violently in Atlanta.

Progress out of 1850 Atlanta has been slow for people of color, but the city has shown the way for much of the nation. Slavery was abolished in 1865, but it took almost one hundred years to pass the Civil Rights Act of 1964, prohibiting discrimination on the basis of race, color, religion, sex or national origin, followed by the Voting Rights Act of 1965, allowing African Americans to exercise their right to vote. This was due in no small part to the leadership and sacrifices of Atlanta's finest citizens, including Dr. Martin Luther King Jr. and John Robert Lewis. Still, equal rights under the law do not ensure equal access to opportunities or equal treatment by society. The struggle for Atlanta's people of color continues.

THE RASCAL DEMBY AND THE RING OF DEPOT ROBBERS

With the murder of McWilliams and the near murder of Alexander Stephens in 1849, both occurring nearly in in the city center, Atlanta's reputation for criminality developed from rampant petty offenses to something more serious and frightening to visitors. However, neither of these incidents could be directly connected to a local bad element or to either of the two most notorious neighborhoods of early Atlanta, Murrell's Row and Snake Nation. The murder of McWilliams was committed by a local, but not an Atlantan, and the incident between Cone and Stephens didn't occur between Atlantans.

The robberies of 1850 changed the last feelings anyone might have had about Atlanta's crime being generally casual or its criminals being under relative control. The city's criminal elements were becoming bolder and more organized and disrupting the city's most important institution, the railroads. The most dastardly and well-organized incident of theft in city history occurred in perfect John Murrell fashion, the infamous namesake for Murrell's Row. The book about Murrell's exploits and methods is very likely to have provided inspiration and instruction to the thieves.

It began at around one o'clock in the morning on April 16, 1850. The night watchman for the Western and Atlantic Railroad discovered fires burning in the warehouses owned by A.W. Wheat (near the present location of Martin Luther King Jr. National Historical Park).

All four buildings owned by Wheat were soon burning violently. The town was lit up by the flames. This was only the beginning of the night's incidents.

About three hours later, another warehouse owned by John F. Mims (later Atlanta's sixth mayor) was found burning. About an hour later, another fire was burning in the cotton warehouse owned by Major Z.A. Rice.

The town was thrown into yet another panic. This was the first major fire in Atlanta history. All four of Wheat's warehouses burned to the ground. Early after daylight, it was learned that these fires were an elaborate distraction to draw the attention of the town and set them into a panic while thieves executed a well-planned robbery. While the last two fires were raging, the thieves broke into the office of the Georgia Railroad through a window and took the money drawer. The drawer was later found underneath one of the trains. The thieves had made off with seventy-five dollars.

It didn't take long to capture some of the perpetrators. The first exposed in the plot were slaves who had been employed by the railroads. When questioned, they revealed a much more elaborate crime ring that had been operating for some time, mainly preying on the railroad depots.

The captured slaves identified three other men as the primary organizers of the crime ring. These were John J. Mulkey, J.W. Demby and a man named H.M. Collins. Demby, Collins and Mulkey were jewelers, and their criminal behavior had not been suspected up to now. A search of the residence Demby and Mulkey owned together revealed a large cache of goods that had been stolen from the railroads over the past several months.

It's not completely known how extensive the robberies were or how many people were involved. Around the same period as the 1850 robberies, a man named Crawford from Snake Nation was caught and prosecuted for having driven a wagon to the back of a store on Whitehall Street and cleaning out everything. It's possible this robbery was connected to the same ring of thieves.

The items were identified by a Mr. Orme, the agent of the Georgia Railroad, to have been stolen from the depot and other buildings. Mulkey and Collins were arrested that day. A posse was organized and dispatched to pursue Demby, who had left the previous Monday with a wagonload of stolen goods to sell in Campbellton. He had already made several trips there to auction stolen goods from the back of a wagon.

One of the slaves involved in the crime was convicted for his participation in the thefts and arson and given forty lashes. Four others confessed as well but were not tried. Their owners agreed to administer punishment once they reached home.

A few days after the fires, the city council established positions for two watchmen to patrol the city from 10:00 p.m. every night until daylight.

One of the first watchmen employed by the city was the former deputy marshal Tom Shivers.

The posse sent for Demby was successful. All three of the accused were brought before Mayor Wyllys Buell days later. Bail for Demby was set at $5,000 ($3,000 for his crimes against the Georgia Railroad and an additional $2,000 for crimes against the Macon and Western Railroad). Mulkey's bail was set at $1,000. H.M. Collins was released due to a lack of evidence against him. Mulkey and Demby were put in the Decatur jail to await the next term of the superior court in Decatur. Demby's bail was later reduced by half, and Mulkey was let out without paying his bail for reasons that are not clear.

Demby didn't stay in the Decatur jail very long and didn't wait around to let the courts decide his fate. By the middle of May, probably after being released on bail, he was back out and fled the city. From Atlanta, he headed south and remained on the run for about a month. A man named J.J. Diamond was sent to hunt him down and apprehended Demby in New Orleans.

Diamond hauled Demby back to Decatur and put him back in jail, but the rascal stayed only about a month. On June 11, 1850, he escaped again. The jailer, his son and another man had entered Demby's cell for some reason and while they were nearer to the center of the room, Demby simply stepped out the door and locked it behind him. There is no more information about the fate of Demby after that. We can only assume that given a second shot at it, he was able to stay hidden and out of the reach of the law the rest of his days.

30

THE ROUSTING OF ATLANTA'S
PROSTITUTES FROM SNAKE NATION

Though crime was rampant in Murrell's Row, the outrage of residents and the Moral Party was principally focused on another Atlanta neighborhood called Snake Nation. Snake Nation was in the southwestern part of town around where Peters Street now passes over the railroad tracks. Today much of what was Snake Nation is in the Castleberry Hill District.

The area was apparently named Snake Nation in refence to the snake oil salesmen who would pass through town and make this area their base of operation. According to one old resident, Isaac Pilgrim, the name commemorated a surprising hunting trip that took place in the area when it was still a thick forest:

> *Old Dad Chapman…and a fellow named Carroll were out hunting in the woods about Peters Street crossing and saw about twenty-five or thirty snakes out there and named the place Snake Nation. When the rag tag of the town settled up Snake Nation, it still kept its name, and it deserved it. It wasn't safe to be caught in Snake Nation after the snakes left and the white folks took possession.*

Much of the news of Snake Nation was chronicled by Cornelius Hanleiter in his letters to the *Georgia Citizen* newspaper in Macon under the pseudonym "Gabriel." He described the reaction the town had toward one of these snake oil salesmen who passed through in 1850:

A certain M(aster) D(rinker) named Star, who professes phrenology, &c., has so annoyed our people, for several weeks past, with his "oligies" and "isms," that it was determined to treat him to a free ride out of town on a single rail! A party was organized and dispatched to Snake Nation in quest of him. But the M.D. having got wind of what was going on, made himself scarce; and the valiant "Greasers" returned without a single laurel. This is much to be regretted in as much as a hundred persons or more, (some of them excessively pious fathers), who had "accidentally" assembled in the neighborhood to see the fun, were most egregiously disappointed!

The reference Hanleiter makes in his letter to the hundred or so "pious fathers" who had "accidentally" gathered in the area is a sly reference to Snake Nation's primary business. Though it was certainly known for its traveling mesmerists, con artists and snake oil salesmen, those were minor distractions compared to Snake Nation's main source of popularity and outrage, prostitution. It was well known that Snake Nation was the place to go if one was in search of a prostitute, and it did a thriving trade in this business.

In 1850, it was estimated that there were around forty prostitutes living in Snake Nation and around thirty more sprinkled throughout the city. That would calculate to a total population of around seventy prostitutes plying their business in a city of about two thousand free people, or nearly 4 percent of the population of the city. This is consistent with an analysis made by Franklin Garrett, Atlanta's most celebrated historian. In Garrett's estimates, he found that the occupation is either left blank or entered as "none" for eighty-five citizens of the city on the census that was performed that year. Among these were many female heads of household who don't appear to be wealthy or widows. Not all of these women may have been prostitutes, but the other options for a single woman to support herself, especially with children, were severely limited. These estimates did not include Black slaves who may have also been part of the city's prostitution. It's difficult to say how many there were, but liaisons between white men and Black slaves are well known to have occurred in the South.

With one prostitute for around every dozen or so men living in the city (though, without doubt, many or most of their clients were passing through on the train and not residents of the city), it seems very likely that many of Atlanta's male citizens were funding steady business in Snake Nation.

In 1888, a reporter from the *Atlanta Constitution* tried to persuade Judge Samuel B. Hoyt, one of Atlanta's early residents, to recount some of what happened in Snake Nation in the late 1840s. The judge divulged some details. Unfortunately, both men deemed these details unfit for publication, saying only, "'The bacchanalian orgies that were carried on in some of the homes in Snake Nation were horrible—unfit to write of. The nameless crimes which were common to that place would fill volumes.' And the judge then went into a few thrilling details, which will never go into print."

In 1850, Atlanta was a city of working-class poor. Among these people, nearly all women had to work in some way their entire adult lives. Obviously, women who supported themselves had to work to survive. This gave them few options. The most common occupation for a woman to support herself in the nineteenth century was as a domestic servant. These jobs would have been far more limited in Atlanta, where slave labor filled most of the need for domestic tasks beyond what was performed by a family.

Opportunities for women were very slowly beginning to emerge in the late 1840s. The first woman to receive a medical degree in the United States, Elizabeth Blackwell, earned her degree in 1849 from Geneva Medical College in New York.

Many of the prostitutes in Atlanta were also immigrants. Some were probably Native Americans, making them less desirable to Americans of this era to be hired as domestic servants. Lack of opportunity led these women eventually into prostitution. Dr. William Sanger was one of few to gather information on the subject in 1859. He interviewed two thousand prostitutes who were serving time in New York's Blackwell's Island Prison. The study revealed that about 75 percent of the women had worked as domestic servants or seamstresses before becoming prostitutes. The last quarter of them were abused or abandoned wives who had been left to their own devices. A quarter of the women were homeless and penniless when they decided to enter the trade. One inmate interviewed summed up her motivation to be a prostitute succinctly: "No work, no money and no home."

As with most other crimes, the enforcement of any laws prohibiting prostitution was halfhearted in Atlanta's early days. When it was punished at all, a rare occurrence, it was treated simply as disorderly conduct and the perpetrator (the prostitute, not the client) was given a light fine. The first Atlanta case involving a pimp was that of a man named John Quick. The only charge brought against him in March 1849 was for keeping his business open on the Sabbath. He was then discharged without even a fine. His only penalty was the payment of his court costs.

On the same day as the case of John Quick, a woman named Elizabeth Carter was also tried for disorderly conduct. It's very likely that the disorderly conduct of which she was being accused was prostitution in cooperation with John Quick. She was ordered to pay a fine of ten dollars and released.

Quick was charged again for the same offense in April 1849 and was again discharged after paying his court costs. Finally, in November of that year, the record made John Quick's true offenses clear and specific. He was found guilty of keeping a "disorderly conduct house" and fined ten dollars. Quick appealed the decision and was denied. Two of John Quick's other associates, Lucinda and Georgiana Burdit, were ordered to appear before the council on this same day but didn't show up. The names of these two women appeared again when the city finally cracked down on prostitution the following summer.

Snake Nation was not solely inhabited by prostitutes and thieves. There were several families living there who had children in the home. There is no indication with any certainty whether these were happy family homes or not. Probably, some were, some weren't. It's clear that the more affluent citizens of the city felt they *weren't* after an incident during March 1850. Two ladies from the "better" parts of Atlanta, whose names we don't know, decided to go on a well-intentioned mission into Snake Nation. They wanted to rescue some of the wayward children of the neighborhood from what seemed to be neglected lives. As Hanleiter put it, they were looking for "a few of the hundreds of dissolute children that swarm our streets and by-ways." They entered Snake Nation and began speaking with some of the children there. Once they were noticed by some of the adult residents, no time was wasted in expelling the intruders. A woman rushed from her house cursing the women and demanding they leave. When the two ladies hesitated, they were pelted with rocks until they beat a hasty retreat out of the neighborhood.

The incident didn't end there. Later that day, the fiancé of one of these presumptuous but well-intentioned ladies appeared at the house of the violent woman in question and loudly demanded that she come out to answer for her offense. Instead, two or three men came out ready for a fight. The fiancé had come prepared though. He drew a revolver and yelled, "The powder and lead in this shooting iron cost me just ten cents, and if anyone interferes to prevent me from punishing this ——, I'll spend the whole amount on him!" After this show of force, the man with the revolver "got his satisfaction." Hanleiter's story of the incident doesn't tell us how. Most likely, the man beat the woman in the street while the men watched helplessly for fear of his revolver.

This incident, as well as the daily outrages of seeing the prostitutes in Snake Nation going about their business finally spurred Mayor Wyllys Buell and the city council to take some action. On July 5, 1850, the city council passed an ordinance to remove the "lewd houses in the southwestern portion of the town." The ordinance also declared that notices must be served by the marshal "to each lewd woman charged with being a nuisance to leave the city in three days and on failure so to do to be removed by the marshal beyond the corporate limits." The next day, the council met to further amend the ordinance to say that the marshal must also seize as much of the property of the person accused as was needed to satisfy any fines or court costs. Second offenses would carry a fine of up to fifty dollars or imprisonment in the calaboose.

Marshal German Lester went to Snake Nation and hauled several prostitutes before the city council. Minutes of the trials of the accused people appeared on July 22, 1850. Some reports given by Cornelius Hanleiter have indicated there were fifteen women accused during this crackdown, but only ten women's names and one man appear in the council minutes. It may be that a courtesy was made to some of the women for some reason by withholding their names from the record. Some of them had appeared before the council already for past offenses. The names appearing in the council minutes on July 22 are Sarah Webster, Catherine Keller, Mahala Seago, Mary Battle, Mary Leach, Georgiana Burdit, Lucinda Button, Georgiana Graham, Emiline Seaton, Washington Goslin and his wife, Sarah Goslin. Some, but not all these names appeared in the 1850 census as citizens of Atlanta. Evidently, John Quick, probably with several others, had made it out of town before he was dragged in by the marshal once again.

The name of the prostitutes Mahala Seago and Mary Leach are interesting ones. Seago is probably the same woman registered as Mahala Vault of Atlanta in the 1850 census. She was twenty-three years old at that time with two daughters in her household, ages three and one. A seven-year-old child named Sarah Leach was also in the residence, probably the daughter of Mary Leach. Mary Leach was a free Black woman of about thirty years of age who must have resided with Mahala but did not appear in the census. There is no other clear information about these women, but the names Mahala and Seago were common Creek names during this time. This woman was probably a Creek still living in Georgia.

Several Atlanta citizens, whose names were not recorded, were also subpoenaed to testify about their first-hand knowledge that these women were, in fact, prostitutes. This must have been quite embarrassing for them. Hanleiter wrote, "There were some scenes of a revolting character; and none more so than to see and hear married men—grey-headed sires of virtuous children—questioned and cross-questioned as to their familiarity with these wantons."

The double standard often associated with prostitution held true in 1850 Atlanta. The prostitutes were charged, convicted and banished from town, but the men who admitted to engaging their services and funding the institution were not considered guilty of anything illegal.

By the end of the trials, according to Hanleiter's summary, fifteen of the women charged were found guilty, all but one of those accused. Marshal Lester then evicted a number of other people living in Snake Nation who were suspected, probably being named by the subpoenaed men. Among them were a few families with children who were expelled from the city.

In the end, the punishment and evictions of the women and their families from Snake Nation was wholly ineffective in ridding Atlanta of prostitution. Probably like John Quick and some of his associates, most of the prostitutes and their pimps or madams simply left town for a while until the trials were over and then returned to their work. A few days later, Snake Nation was practicing its primary trade once again with open impunity for the city's ordinances. The more upright citizens of the city continued to rail against the mayor and council for their ineffectiveness in stemming the tide of overall misconduct.

31

MAYOR NORCROSS

Atlanta was now an overgrown town with none of the marks of a city. Its streets were unpaved and such a thing as a sewer was unheard of. One marshal and his assistant were the police force.
—George Gilman Smith

The population was a conglomeration of railroad hands out of employment, and gambling of daily occurrence, with an occasional murder.
—Charles Wubner

As 1850 progressed into the hot months, patience diminished. People stayed out on the streets during all hours. Along with the more minor crimes practiced out in the open like gambling and prostitution, the city had just made national headlines for an outbreak of smallpox, its first attempted murder, closely followed by its first actual murder, followed by the discovery of an organized crime ring in its midst and a very serious incident of arson.

In the face of this, Jonathan Norcross saw the time was right for his Moral Party to take over the leadership of Atlanta. He accepted a nomination for mayor after a mass meeting held in early 1850. He had lost the first election in 1848 to Moses Formwalt and the Free and Rowdy Party, but times had certainly changed. He and other business leaders fanned the flames of the city's frustration, making campaign speeches and lambasting their opposition in the *Weekly Intelligencer*, the newspaper they had bought from Cornelius

Hanleiter. It was time for Atlanta to put aside its adolescent foolishness and become a city. As part of their platform of renewed virtue, they handed out apples and candy instead of the usual whiskey and gin.

Norcross's opponents in the Free and Rowdy Party were still very formidable. For their candidate, they nominated Leonard C. Simpson, a lawyer and former member of the city council. The Moral Party had lost every election in Atlanta thus far (three times). The Free and Rowdy Party was less organized, but it represented more of the common hearts and minds of the citizens of Atlanta.

As the election approached, it became apparent to everyone that this one was not shaping up like the others. Norcross and the Moral Party were running an effective campaign. Violence in Five Points and along Decatur Street escalated as the Rowdy supporters tried to bully their way to another victory. G.G. Smith recalled there were daily fights in the streets, and at night the city "seemed to be in the possession of a howling mob." Many of the Rowdies vented their anger at Norcross. Smith noted, "Jonathan was known to be uncompromising in his hatred to liquor and disorder."

As 1850 drew to a close and Election Day approached, the Rowdies began to formulate new rationales for their continued defiance. As Thomas Martin put it, "Even in the face of a win for the Moral Party, the Rowdies planned open defiance to the city." Many of them were saying that "Uncle Jonathan" would find the town "too hot to hold him" if he won the election or tried to institute his proposed reforms.

Election Day, January 20, 1851, was even more excited and violent than the past years. More than sixty fights took place on Decatur Street between sunup and well past sundown. As was often the case, G.G. Smith took the time to write an interesting description of what happened next: "I was in the store where I clerked, on Whitehall Street, when the Marshal, William McConnell, came hurriedly to the door and said to Mr. McPherson, 'I summon you to go to Decatur Street to suppress a riot.' There was open war."

When all the votes were counted, Norcross and the Moral Party won the day. This was not the end of the final battle for control of Atlanta. It was the beginning. As Norcross took office as the fourth mayor in the City of Atlanta, according to Cornelius Hanleiter, "Threats against the new mayor were freely uttered." Rumors ran wild that some of the worst characters from Murrell's Row were planning to get themselves arrested so that they could appear before the mayor and kill him there in the council chambers. These rumors may not have been taken entirely seriously, but that is, in fact, exactly what happened.

In these days, the mayor also served as the justice of the peace for the city. Court was held on the second floor of the McDaniel, Mitchell and Hulsey building on the northeast corner of Whitehall and Hunters Streets. Three months after Norcross took office, a particularly bold ruffian charged with disorderly conduct was brought upstairs to appear before Judge Norcross. It was rumored that the Rowdies had made plans for this confrontation, and supporters from both sides crowded into the courtroom to see the drama unfold. The man was quickly found guilty. Before he could be ushered out of the room, he produced a large knife from the back of his shirt and declared that he was going to turn the courtroom "into a slaughter pen" (a pen a butcher would use to trap animals like hogs to slaughter them). It's hard to believe a wanted criminal could get hold of a large knife while standing before a judge. One of his Rowdy comrades must have somehow slipped it to him unnoticed.

He raised the knife in the air and began slashing left and right with it. The spectators who had gathered started scrambling pell-mell for the door and down the stairs. The man went for the mayor. As Norcross put it, "I didn't stand on dignity a bit, and by the time I got well entrenched behind a big chair, the house was emptied." One of the few left in the room was Allen Johnson, the former DeKalb County sheriff, who was universally acknowledged to have the "bravery of a lion." (He was also the person you might recall, who tried to get ownership of Land Lot 77—most of downtown Atlanta—through a very dubious legal challenge). Before the man could get to Norcross, he was disarmed by well-placed whack from Johnson's hickory cane. Johnson was then assisted by City Marshal William McConnel, his deputy Benjamin Williford and a private citizen named Cicero Strong. They hustled the lout out of the room and propelled him down the steps. They were met by a frantic crowd once they came out the doors and out into the street.

Somehow, in the crush of the crowd—probably assisted by other Rowdies—the man was able to get free of Johnson and Strong and run off into the darkness.

Once the new mayor and council were installed, Decatur made it clear that its patience had run out with its unruly neighbor in the annual address to the grand jury. The city leaders demanded that Atlanta take over jurisdiction of its own criminal court. Norcross and Atlanta were on their own to solve their own problems.

32

THE BRIEF RISE AND FALL OF THE HIGHER LAW PARTY

The incident in the council chambers kicked off several days of violence in Atlanta. The final showdown for the control of the city began on a Thursday. It would end with fire, violence and the Moral Party at last in firm control of the city. The story of Atlanta's development changed drastically in one fateful night.

The intimidation tactics of the Rowdies seem to have succeeded with at least one person. Marshal McConnell quit the job and was replaced by German Lester in February. Mayor Norcross made it clear he was not going to back down to the Rowdies. He planned to deliver on the widespread city reforms he had promised during his mayoral campaign. The rabble of Atlanta didn't plan to back down either. They were seething and scheming for another confrontation with Uncle Jonathan.

While carousing in the bars, a group of Rowdies, including one energetic leader who felt particularly wronged by the city and its government, devised a new plan to overthrow the new city administration and the overbearing Moral Party. It was clear to them now, they thought, that the time of the Free and Rowdy Party was over. They needed a new movement and a new party. They needed a new position that better reflected their views. The rigid Moral Party made it seem like the Free and Rowdy Party was in favor of outright lawlessness. They weren't. They never were. They operated by the general moral code of mankind, not the whims of a few uptight men in Atlanta. They new party they formed on that premise was called the Higher Law Party.

In this way, the tension over the issue of slavery found its way once again into the fight for control of Atlanta. There were none who openly opposed slavery, though they may have in private. The Higher Law Party was at least in one way inspired by the northern abolitionists. One of the laws that had been recently passed as part of the Clay Compromise of 1850, the only substantive concession to the South, had greatly strengthened the requirements that non-slave states enforce the laws of the South by pursuing and returning escaped slaves. Some in the North attempted to reject the law under a defense that there was a "higher law" of human justice. This defense actually succeeded in a handful of cases at this point and was fueling the latest outrage in the South.

On Thursday April 18, 1851, the Higher Law Party felt it had gained enough support and it was time to make an official declaration a week after the man tried to kill Norcross in the council chambers. A man named Pinkney Anderson stepped forward to lead them and declared the independence of the Higher Law Party from the laws of Atlanta. He was supported by Tom Shivers, the former deputy marshal who had been dismissed from his position before finishing his one-year term in 1848. The members of their group would be subject to law of the land, not the city. In the new era of the Higher Law Party, unjust attempts to govern would simply be rejected by the people as they always had been in Atlanta, in Marthasville before that and in Terminus before that. Marshal Lester challenged them in the street, and there was a violent scuffle.

With the help of a group of supportive citizens, Marshal Lester managed to arrest Pinkney Anderson and stuff him in the calaboose. Consistent with their pledge to defy the authority of the city, Tom Shivers went with several others from the Higher Law Party and freed Anderson. The log building that acted as the city's little jail was a pathetic thing. It was like a big upturned wooden crate sitting on the ground and there was no regular guard on duty to watch it, even while it was occupied. In the past, friends of the prisoners inside had been able to lift it up on its side and allow those inside to escape. In this case, Shivers pried some of the logs out and let Pinkney Anderson escape.

Following this escape, there was another confrontation in the street, and this time Marshal Lester was forced to make another temporary retreat. He then went through the city summoning up a posse. The confrontation of Marshal Lester's posse and the Higher Law leaders was vividly recounted by Judge Samuel B. Hoyt to a reporter in 1888:

These bold men had defied the Marshal and the mayor summoned a posse comitatus to arrest the outlaws and imprison them. It was almost impossible to get citizens to serve. They were afraid that these desperate characters all of whom were armed would shoot them down. There was a reign of terror in Marthasville [sic]. It was a critical time in the history of the town. The question was who should rule, the decent people or the outlaws?

At length Marshal Lester succeeded in finding three men as brave ever breathed to assist him in making the arrest. They were Allen E. Johnson, A. Addison and a young Virginian…John T. Wilson. In company with Marshal [Lester] those men set out to capture the roughs. They decided to arrest the leader first. He was a powerful and desperate man. They found him in a groggery….He was armed to the teeth. There were a number of other bad characters in the barroom. Wilson said to Lester, "Who do you want arrested?" Mr. Lester pointed out the tall offender. The bystanders expected to see Wilson killed on the spot, and were very much horrified when the brave young man deliberately marched into the saloon, and without exhibiting a tremor, laid his hand on the big leader's shoulders and quietly said, "You are now my prisoner." To the astonishment of everybody the man glared upon Wilson for a moment, and then quietly submitted to arrest. He was marched away with Wilson on one side of him and Allen Johnson on the other.

This time, they didn't put Anderson in the calaboose. They took him directly to Mayor Norcross. Anderson was given the option to pay bail instead of being locked up once again. Still defiant of the city's authority, he refused to pay, so Norcross ordered Anderson locked in the guardhouse instead of the calaboose. Guards were posted outside to make certain he didn't escape.

As the marshal and a few others went to lock up Anderson again, Tom Shivers met them in the street with a gang of Higher Law followers. They demanded Anderson be set free. There was another violent clash. Weapons were drawn. It became a standoff. Shivers and the Higher Law gang were able to get custody of Anderson from the marshal and his posse but agreed to pay bail for him and appear before the mayor the next day. Surprisingly, they both appeared before Mayor Norcross the following morning. It's not recorded, but very likely a posse was sent to make certain the men appeared as promised the night before. Anderson was fined thirty dollars and Shivers fifty dollars for having set Anderson free the first time and attempting to do it again during the second confrontation.

Shivers and Anderson never paid their fines and went back to stirring up more trouble for Marshal Lester and the mayor. The Higher Law movement had not been broken. The mayor and council appeared weak. The showdown was far from over. They continued to loudly profess their defiance of authority with chants, singing and mock praying in the streets. It began to spread into a riot. Marshal Lester withdrew from the scene once again, and the Higher Law crowd took over the city, loudly carousing and celebrating their victory late into the night.

A group of Higher Law followers went to Decatur and stole the cannon that had been used in the conflict with the Creeks in 1836. They positioned it directly in front of Jonathan Norcross's store on Decatur Street with a note demanding that he leave town or vacate his office. If he did not do so, they would fire it through the front of his store. While they drank and celebrated their apparent victory, they loaded the little cannon with dirt and fired it three times into the front of Norcross's store. This made a mess but caused no significant damage.

On Saturday morning, finding the cannon in front of his store with its threatening note, Norcross took action. Enough was enough. He called a secret, emergency meeting of the city council. They agreed to allocate $200, and the mayor issued a proclamation that all law-abiding citizens were summoned to present themselves for a volunteer police force. Twenty-five men were hand-picked and armed with guns. They were led by William McPherson and Alexander Weldon Mitchell.

The force of twenty-five was also supported by patrols who armed themselves with whatever was handy. They drilled throughout the day and prepared to meet the Higher Law Party that evening when they would be expected out boasting and singing once again. The cannon in front of Norcross's store remained where it was. More than 100 people guarded it to prevent further mischief from the Higher Law crowd.

While the volunteer police force drilled during the day, the Higher Law Party met and set up their own war offices in a boardinghouse on Decatur Street in Murrell's Row. By midnight on Saturday, the Higher Law Party had not emerged. The mayor's police decided to go on the offensive. They split into several squads and went on the move to the boarding house and several other parts of the city where they knew the rebels were hiding. William McPherson and Alexander Weldon Mitchell led the squad to the headquarters of the Higher Law Party.

As the mayor's police approached the house, armed and ready, most of the Higher Law Party broke from cover and ran, disappearing into the night.

Around twenty of them were too slow to flee and became surrounded inside by the volunteer police. The Higher Law Party surrendered and came out one by one to be put into custody.

Among those arrested were Tom Shivers and Pinkney Anderson. Once again, William Harris (Tom Shivers's next-door neighbor), George Humphries and a man named Campbell were also arrested. They filled both the guard house and the calaboose with prisoners and brought the worst before Mayor Norcross once again. There is a record from around 1850 or 1851 of a mass escape from the calaboose where so many were held there that the lot of them, along with comrades outside, were able to lift the entire calaboose off the ground and let everyone out. This probably occurred on the night in April when half the town was in revolt. A new, sturdier calaboose was finally built after this incident, and it served Atlanta until 1865. Humphries's case was dismissed for lack of evidence. The other four were fined to the full extent possible and refused to pay their fines; they were held until the next meeting of the next county superior court in Decatur.

The Higher Law movement was broken, but the Moral Party still did not have control of the city. The final chapter about to unfold was the most violent and chaotic of all.

THE FIRST HOSTILE BURNING
OF ATLANTA

S ome of the deputized or self-deputized citizens were not yet satisfied. At some point soon after the Higher Law Party had been suppressed (whether it was that day or soon after is unclear), a group of them gathered together to decide how they would now deal with the rest of the city. The thrill of action and the encouragement of victory must have still been running hot in their veins. The law had tried to deal fairly with the open prostitution in Snake Nation and the brazen criminals in Murrell's Row and only now had begun to make a difference. The rabble of the most corrupted areas remained. Until they were dealt with, the city still belonged to them, not the Moral Party or the mayor and his council.

This time, the vigilante mob would make certain the city would be rid of them for good. Before venturing out, many of them put on hoods to cover their identities. This was called "white capping." White capping was rare in 1851 but became increasingly common leading up to the Civil War and especially afterward. It began when rough cities like Atlanta would organize to take action as vigilantes to uphold a moral code. Later, during Reconstruction, it increasingly targeted freed African Americans, especially farmers trying to work land alongside white farmers. White capping formed the roots of organized racism and hate groups like the Ku Klux Klan.

They first organized themselves as if preparing a military attack on Snake Nation. At the signal of one of their leaders, "they drew arms, axes and torches, shot, burned and destroyed." They went into the homes of various men, women and children and dragged them into the streets. The men were whipped. All of them were brought miles from town and ordered never to return.

Unlike the last time Snake Nation had been invaded just to reestablish itself days later, the vigilantes took pains to make certain the banished wouldn't return. They went from house to house and tore them down with axes and burned them to the ground. "At dawn, only ashes marked the section where Snake Nation stood."

Even then, their night's work wasn't finished. The white caps then went to Murrell's Row and Slabtown and carried out more personal justice. From that night, on or close to Sunday, April 14, 1851, Atlanta's three notorious neighborhoods never rose again. The volunteer police force was kept in commission for some time after the events of that night but was never recalled out into mass duty.

The drama concerning the defiance of the Higher Law Party, the organizing of the volunteer police and the violence and destruction of the white caps are recorded in newspaper accounts and personal recollections of some of the witnesses, but none of it is recorded in the minutes of the city council. There is only a veiled reference to the events in a letter Jonathan Norcross read to the council on April 11, 1851. While events were still unfolding, he ordered it to be published in the *Weekly Intelligencer*, the newspaper he partially owned. It refers to the first arrest of Pinkney and Shivers.

Atlanta, April 11, 1851
To the Board of Council

Gentlemen: Allow me if you please to call your attention to some matters connected with our city police. While I thank you for your encouragement and support to me in the discharge of any ordinary and sometimes painful duties during the short time I have been in office. This note is addressed to you for the purpose of bringing to your notice the names of others. I mention first certain services rendered the marshals in discharge of their duty by our fellow citizen Mr. Allen Johnson on the occasion of a recent attempt to resist the city authorities. I mention also the services of our fellow citizen Mr. W.H. Forsyth on a similar but former occasion. I need not particularize in these cases. Suffice it to say they both rendered that kind of service and exhibited that kind of spirit without the exercise of which, on some occasions law and order would be trampled under foot.

I am aware that it is the duty of every citizen to uphold law and all necessary authority and while we have no reason to doubt the good will and firm purpose of every good citizen to do this I think it not improper to express our appreciation in an official manner in such cases as those in which Mr. Johnson and Mr. Forsyth took part. There are other citizens who deserve our thanks for their assistance on the same occasions and I regret I am not in possession of the necessary facts to enable me to distinguish their names.

Yours respectfully, J. Norcross, Mayor

Norcross's letter to the Council about the incident is vague and intentionally incomplete. It is doubtful he was unaware of the names of other people who were involved as he claims in the letter; more likely he did not want to divulge the names. Several of the events that occurred after April 11 are described in a newspaper article but none is recorded in city documents. Other accounts of the incident are similarly vague. Perhaps that is for good reason. One unnamed participant in the raid commented, "In later years, one of the raiders said he doubted if the true story of that 'night of terror' would ever be told, as it was one every man involved wanted to forget."

Recollecting the defiance he faced and the actions taken by the city and its citizens, Norcross later said, "From that day to this no good officer of the city has ever lacked the assistance or encouragement due him by the citizens of Atlanta in the enforcement of law and order within its limits."

Atlanta had changed forever.

After the violent events of 1851, the Free and Rowdy Party never won another election in Atlanta. In 1852, Thomas Gibbs, representing the Moral Party, became mayor. Jonathan Norcross served on the city council. The next three elections had no party affiliation. By 1855, the elections had shifted to a Whig versus Democrat race like national politics.

Word of Pinkney Anderson and the Atlanta Higher Law Party was not heard again. Tom Shivers continued to play a prominent role in the city. He even built back a reputation and regained his position as deputy marshal in 1862 serving under Marshal Benjamin Williford. In 1863, Shivers was killed in a gunfight in front of Muhlenbrink's Saloon on Whitehall Street by G. Whitfield Anderson, a rival for the position of deputy marshal. Anderson was found not guilty on the grounds of self-defense. Shivers, the witnesses claimed, drew first.

CONCLUSION

Antebellum Atlanta was a city of drunks and thieves. I doubt that was a conscious career choice for any of them though. Every one of those drunks and thieves in 1800s Atlanta started as a railroad worker I suspect, a profession that would not attract people with a lot of options for other employment. Once the railroad work went away, there wasn't much else to do. They weren't forced to become lawbreakers, but in the aggregate, it's not surprising that a city with a young, unsophisticated population where jobs were declining ended up with a lot of crime.

Atlanta was also a town full of prostitutes. The circumstances that led to this are easier to evaluate because there were so few options for these people. I think it's fair to say that in almost every case, the women who turned to that profession had no other way to survive. There were no jobs in Atlanta for maids or nannies or seamstresses. The amount of money one could earn from washing and ironing, seemingly the only job available for females in early Atlanta, was not enough to support any children. I would love to know the story of Mahala Seago and Mary Leach. They were both prostitutes and both single mothers who shared a house in Snake Nation. Mary was a free Black woman who had a seven-year-old daughter named Sarah in 1850. Mahala had two daughters: Lana, three years old, and Mary, one year old. She was also probably a Creek. How did Mary and Mahala find each other and end up in Atlanta? How did Mary gain her freedom? Why was Mahala not with the other Creeks in the West? Why was she left behind, alone? It's hard to read about Mary and Mahala and feel anything other than sympathy for these unfortunate women—not judgment for their crimes.

Then there are the town officials. In particular, there was Jonathan Norcross. The descriptions in this book have called him a man of extreme intelligence and talent who lived according to a strict moral code. It was never said here that he seemed altogether nice. The settlement of Atlanta and much of the reason it was successful in its early years can be attributed to Norcross more than any other person. He had more of a vision for the city than anyone else and was amazingly effective in carrying it out. Norcross made a proposal in 1847 that Atlanta should become the capitol of Georgia. 1847! He was laughed at. Hogs and cows were still using the downtown area as a pasture in 1847. There were still trees growing in the middle of the roads. Yet this man already had a vision of how important the city would become that he was willing to announce publicly, knowing he would be scoffed at by most people. He was planning for the future. He knew there would be a day when the same people would no longer laugh at the idea, and they would remember who had the foresight to first say it.

Norcross's vision wasn't for all the citizens of Atlanta. He hated Andrew Jackson, but I see much of the same view of the world in Norcross that I see in Andrew Jackson. They each had a firm, clear vision for growth in the United States. People who didn't fit into that vision were to be removed. There is no proof that Norcross organized or condoned the vigilante mob rule that took place in Atlanta in 1851. It seems likely though. He certainly organized the volunteer police force to put down the near rebellion of the Higher Law mob, which was an appropriate thing for a mayor to do. Many people in the city certainly wanted the cleaning up of the city to continue from there, and Norcross was a man of action. The unruliest elements of the town were ruthlessly overpowered during Norcross's administration. That much we know. Further conjecture is only that.

More than anyone else, the changes for people of color in Atlanta since 1850 are clearly visible, from the enslaved conditions of the people who literally built the city to today. While the opportunities have improved enormously, they began from a place of oppression that went far beyond what is easily seen on the surface or written into law. The struggle to ensure truly equal access to opportunity for people of color in Atlanta continues as a core element of the city's character.

Atlanta has come a long way since 1851. The metro area supports nearly 6 million people, and it is one of the best places to live in America. The airport is the busiest in the world, moving over 100 million passengers

Locomotives steaming to and from the Atlanta depot. *Library of Congress*.

through Atlanta every year. There is more train traffic in Georgia than ever, and Atlanta is still one of the major hubs for freight moving through the South. Trains are often overlooked these days but remain at the heart of the city. No home in Atlanta or its outlying towns like Decatur is out of earshot of the regular, resonant horn blasts of big diesel locomotives passing many times each day on the same paths laid out so long ago.

The beautiful city that exists now owes a debt of remembrance and respect to all the people who came to that same place across thousands of years; to the people who put much of their life's work into creating the city and creating the railroads that led to it, some willingly, some not; and to all the people who planted a stake in Sandtown, in Standing Peachtree, in Deantown, in Terminus, in Marthasville and in Atlanta.

BIBLIOGRAPHY

Ackerman Lithr. *General map of the Orange & Alexandria Rail Road and its connections north, south, and west.* 1851. Library of Congress. loc.gov.

Acts of the State of Georgia. Milledgeville, GA: Miller Grieve, 1848.

Akers, Trasen Solesmont. *Chilly McIntosh and the Muscogee (Creek) Nation: 1800–1875.* Oklahoma City: Self-published, 2018.

Atkins, Robert, and Griffin Atkins. *Geologic Guide to Panola Mountain State Park.* Georgia Department of Natural Resources, Environmental Protection Division and Georgia Geologic Survey, 1977.

Atlanta City Council Minutes, 1848–1851. Atlanta History Center, Atlanta, Georgia.

Atlanta Constitution. April 22, 1993.

———. "Southern Confederacy." February 3, 1863.

Atlanta History Center. *Native Lands: Indian and Georgia; Creek National Council, Tuckabatchee, 1824.* 2019 exhibit.

"Atlanta Iron Works." *Constitutionalist and Republic* 5, no. 119 (October 1851).

Atlanta Journal. "Recollections of an Atlanta Boy." October 16, 1909.

Atlanta Journal Constitution. June 10, 1934.

Atlanta Weekly Intelligencer. May 26, 1859.

Barnum, P.T. *Struggles and Triumphs; or, Forty Years' Recollections of P.T. Barnum.* Buffalo, NY: Courier Company, 1883.

Bartoletti, Susan Campbell. *Black Potatoes: The Story of the Great Irish Famine, 1845–1850.* New York: Houghton Mifflin, 2001.

Campanella, Richard. *Bienville's Dilemma: A Historical Geography of New Orleans.* Lafayette: University of Louisiana Press Lafayette, 2008.

Carr, Thomas, Thomas Williamson and David Schwimmer. "A New Genus of Tyrannosauroid from the Late Cretaceous (Middle Campanian) Demopolis Formation of Alabama." *Journal of Vertebrate Paleontology* 25, no. 1 (1997): 118–43.

Central of Georgia Railway Records. *Right Way* magazines. cofga.org/railway/history.

A Century of Lawmaking for a New Nation: U.S. Congressional Documents and Debates, 1774–1875, Statutes at Large, 21st Congress, 1st Session, 1830.

Columbus Times. "Boston Again." April 22, 1851.

———. "The Boston Nullification." March 4, 1851.

Cotterill, R.S. "Railroads and Western Trade." *Mississippi Valley Historical Review* 3, no. 4 (March 1917): 427–41.

Daily Chronicle & Sentinel. April 25, 1851.

———. September 8, 1845.

———. September 14, 1848.

Daily Morning News. April 29, 1850.

———. December 30, 1850.

DeKalb County Historical Society information files.

DeKalb County Superior Court Records, 1836–1843. Dekalb County History Center, Decatur, Georgia.

Derrick, Samuel Melanchthon. *Centennial History of South Carolina Railroad*. Spartanburg, SC: Reprint Company, 1975. Originally published 1930.

Dickens, Roy Jr., and James McKinley. *Frontiers in the Soil: The Archaeology of Georgia*. Athens, GA: Carl Vinson Institute of Government, 2003.

Digital Archaeological Record. "The Live Oak Quarry: Soapstone Ridge, Georgia." https://core.tdar.org.

Dr. John H. Goff Collection, Georgia Department of Archives and History. Morrow, Georgia.

Elliott, Daniel T. *The Live Oak Soapstone Quarry*. Atlanta: Garrow & Associates, 1986.

Etheridge, Robbie. *Creek Country*. Chapel Hill: University of North Carolina Press, 2003.

———. "English Trade in Deerskins and Indian Slaves." New Georgia Encyclopedia, https://www.georgiaencyclopedia.org.

Fears, Darryl. "Seeking More Than Apologies for Slavery." *Washington Post*, June 20, 2005.

Federal censuses, 1850–1870.

Federal Union. "News from Atlanta." October 10, 1848.

———. "A Reward Offered for Terrell." October 10, 1848.

Felton, Rebecca Latimer. *Country Life in Georgia in the Days of My Youth*. Atlanta: Index Printing Company, 1919.

Gabriel [Cornelius Hanleiter]. Letter from Atlanta. *Georgia Citizen*, July 23, 1850.

———. Letter from Atlanta. *Georgia Citizen*. March 10, 1850.

Garrett, Franklin M. *Atlanta and Environs: A Chronicle of Its People and Events*. Vol. 1. Athens: University of Georgia Press, 1969.

———. "Chapter 29 1851." *Atlanta Historical Bulletin* 12, no. 4 (December 1967): 102.

Georgia Citizen. April 17, 1850.

———. April 25, 1850.

———. August 5, 1850.

———. August 30, 1850.

———. "Higher Law Nonsense." June 14, 1851.

———. July 9, 1850.

———. July 23, 1850.

———. September 5, 1850.

Georgia Constitutionalist, January 28, 1836.

Georgia Journal and Messenger. April 24, 1850.

———. September 20, 1848.

Georgia Railroad Chronical and Sentinel. September 8, 1845.

Gordon, John Steele. *An Empire of Wealth: The Epic History of American Economic Power*. New York: Harper Perennial, 2005.

Hain, Steven. *The Invention of the Creek Nation, 1670–1763*. Lincoln: University of Nebraska Press, 2014.

Hanleiter's Atlanta City Directory for 1871. Atlanta: William R. Hanleiter, Publisher, 1871.

Hemperley, Marion R. *Historic Indian Trails of Georgia*. Athens: Garden Club of Georgia, 1989.

Hergesheimer, E. *Map Showing the Distribution of the Slave Population of the Southern States of the United States*. Compiled from the census of Washington Henry S. Graham, 1861. Map. www.loc.gov/item/99447026.

Hill, Andrew T. "The Second Bank of the United States." Federal Reserve History, federalreservehistory.org.

Holmes, William F. "Whitecapping in Late Nineteenth Century Georgia." In *From the Old South to the New: Essays on the Transitional South*, 123. Westport, CT: Greenwood Press, 1981.

Houston, James Johnston. *Western & Atlantic Railroad of the State of Georgia, Atlanta*. Atlanta: Georgia Public Service Commission, 1931.

Hoyt, S.B. "The Shumate Family; The Story of Some of the Pioneers of DeKalb County." *Atlanta Constitution*, 1886.

Indian Affairs: Laws and Treaties, vol. 2, *Treaties*. Treaty with the Creeks, 1825.

Irvine, William Stafford. "Terminus and Deanville." *Atlanta Historical Bulletin* 3, no. 13 (April 1938): 103.

Jabour, Anya. "Women's Work and Sex Work in Nineteenth-Century America" *Mercy Street Revealed* (blog), Georgia Public Broadcasting. pbs.org.

Jackson County Historical Society News 16, no. 1.

Jackson, Edwin L., and Mary E. Stakes. *The Georgia Studies Book: Our State and the Nation*. Athens: University of Georgia, Carl Vinson Institute of Government, 2004.

Kappler, Charles J. *Indian Affairs: Laws and Treaties; Treaty with the Creeks, 1825*. Washington, D.C.: Government Printing Office, 1904.

Kelly, Arthur, and Larry Meier, Larry. "A Pre-Agricultural Village Site in Fulton County, Georgia." *Proceeding of the Southeastern Archaeological Conference* Bulletin No. 11 (1969).

Kurtz, Wilbur. "The Story of Land Lot 77." *Atlanta Historical Bulletin* 8, no. 32 (December 1947): 46.

Kurtz, Wilbur, and Laurie Kurtz. "The Kurtz Chronicles of Early Atlanta." *Atlanta Historical Journal* 26, no. 1 (1982).

Lane, Mills. *The Rambler in Georgia*. Savannah, GA: Beehive Press, 1973.

Lehrman Institute. "Andrew Jackson, Banks and the Panic of 1836." https:// lehrmaninstitute.org/history/Andrew-Jackson-1837.html.

Letters written by Lt. Edward Deas to C.A. Harris, Superintendent of Indian Affairs, last dated January 23, 1837; Letter to Bob Aldrich, dated February 14, 2018, from Professor Christopher D. Haveman. University of West Alabama. Livingston, Alabama.

Library of Congress. "Compromise of 1850: Primary Documents in American History." https://guides.loc.gov/compromise-1850.

———. "The Public Statutes at Large of the United States of America from the Organization of the Government in 1780, to March 3, 1845." www. loc.gov/law/help/statutes-at-large.

Martin, Thomas. *Atlanta and Its Builders*. N.p.: Century Memorial Publishing Company, 1902.

Massey, Dr. R.J. "Reminiscences of Old Decatur Street." *Atlanta Georgian and News*, February 11, 1909.

———. *Weekly Constitution*. April 24, 1883.

McConnell, J. *McConnell's Historical Maps of the United States*. Chicago: McConnell Map Company, 1919.

McKenny, Thomas, James Hall, Hatherly Todd and Joseph Todd. *History of the Indian Tribes of North America: With Biographical Sketches and Anecdotes of the Principal Chiefs*. Philadelphia: D. Rice & Company, 1872.

Meyer, David. "The Roots of American Industrialization, 1790–1860." Economic History Association, http://eh.net.

Mills, Quincy T. *Cutting Along the Color Line: Black Barbers and Barber Shops in America*. Philadelphia: University of Pennsylvania Press, 2013.

National Park Service. "Horseshoe Bend National Historic Site," nps.gov.

Nicholson, Gilbert. "Did Delta Hub Propel Atlanta over Birmingham?" *Birmingham Business Journal*, April 27, 2003.

Nohemi Sala, Juan Luis Arsuaga, Ana Pantoja-Pérez, Adrián Pablos, Ignacio Martínez, Rolf M. Quam, Asier Gómez-Olivencia, José María Bermúdez de Castro and Eudald Carbonell. "Lethal Interpersonal Violence in the Middle Pleistocene." *PLoS One* 10 no. 5 (2015).

Norcross, Jonathan. *The History of Democracy*. New York: G.P. Putnam & Sons, 1884.

———. "The History of Democracy: Considered as a Party Name and as a Political Organization." *North Georgia Citizen*, September 2, 1909.

O'Dea, Aaron et al. "Formation of the Isthmus of Panama." Science Advances 2, no. 8 (2016).

Owens, Emily Alyssa. "Fantasies of Consent: Black Women's Sexual Labor in 19th Century New Orleans." PhD diss., Harvard University, 2015.

Peebles, Jennifer. "Here's Where Irish People Live in Georgia." *Atlanta Journal Constitution*. March 16, 2017.

Personal Letters of Andrew Jackson (1814)

Phillips, Betsy. "One Thumb Up! Severed 200-Year-Old Thumb Sticks Out at the Tennessee State Museum." Nashville Scene, nashvillescene.com.

Poor, Henry V. *History of the Railroad and Canals of the United States*. Vol. 1. New York: J.H. Schultz, 1860.

President Jackson's Veto Message Regarding the Bank of the United States; July 10, 1832, The Avalon Project, Yale Law School Lillian Goldman Law Library.

Price, Vivian. *Historic Dekalb County: An Illustrated History*. San Antonio, TX: Historical Publishing Network, 2008.

———. *History of DeKalb County, Georgia, 1822–1900*. Fernandina Beach, FL: Wolfe Publishing Company, 1997.

Quinn, Christopher. "Much of Georgia's Story Written by Irish." *Atlanta Journal-Constitution*, 2014.

Ramey Berry, Daina (guest), Leslie Harris (guest) and Joan Neuberger. "Urban Slavery in the Antebellum United States." *15 Minute History Podcast* (2014).

Records of the U.S. Senate, National Archives and Records Administration.

Reed, Merl Elwyn. "Louisiana's Transportation Revolution: The Railroad, 1830–1850." Louisiana State University, 1957.

Register of Free Persons of Color, Freedman Record, Inferior Court of Dekalb County, 1851–1864.

Rezneck, Samuel. "The Social History of an American Depression, 1837–1843." *American Historical Review* 40, no. 4 (1935): 662–87.

Roberts, Alasdair. *America's First Great Depression: Economic Crisis and Political Disorder after the Panic of 1837*. Ithaca, NY: Cornell University Press, 2012.

Savannah Daily Republican. August 11, 1851.

Savannah Morning News. September 2, 1850.

Scheiber, Harry N. "The Pet Banks in Jacksonian Politics and Finance, 1833–1841." *Journal of Economic History* 23, no. 2 (1963): 196–214.

Smith, George Gilman. Transcriptions of Diaries of George Gilman Smith and "My Life Story" in the George Gilman Smith Books, #971-z. Southern Historical Collection, The Wilson Library, University of North Carolina at Chapel Hill.

Smith, Thomas Ruys. "The John A. Murrell Conspiracy and the Lynching of the Vicksburg Gamblers in Literature." *Mississippi Quarterly* 59, nos. 1–2 (Winter 2005).

Smithers, Gregory. *Native Southerners: Indigenous History from Origins to Removal*. Norman: University of Oklahoma Press, 2019.

Southern Miscellany. October 14, 1843.

Southern Recorder. August 2, 1836.

Stanyard, William. "A Technical Summary of Georgia Prehistory" TRC Garrow Associates, http://www.oocities.org/wfstanyard/gach.htm.

Stewart, Virgil. *History of the Detection, Conviction, Life and Designs of John A. Murrell, the Great Western Land Pirate*. Athens: Republished by G. White, Tennessee, 1835.

Summer, David E. "Everybody's Cousin: John J. Thrasher Was one of Atlanta's Founder and Most Colorful Figure" *Georgia Historical Quarterly* 84, no. 2 (Summer 2000): 295–307.

Swanton, John R. *Early History of the Creek Indians and Their Neighbors*. Smithsonian Institution Bureau of American Ethnology Bulletin 73. Washington, D.C.: Government Printing Office, 1922.

Thomas, Henry Walter. *Digest of the Railroad Laws of Georgia*. Atlanta: Franklin Printing and Publishing Company, 1895.

Trotti, Louis Haygood. *The DeKalb Historical Society's Year Book, 1952*. Decatur Public Library, DeKalb County, Georgia.

University of Texas Arlington. "A Continent Divided: Zachary Taylor." https://library.uta.edu.

U.S. Census Bureau Annual Estimates of the Resident Population: April 1, 2010 to July 1, 2018. Metropolitan and Micropolitan Statistical Area; and for Puerto Rico 2018 Population Estimates.

U.S. Department of Commerce/Bureau of the Census. Population of the Standard Metro Area: 1970 to 1960. 1970 Census of Population.

Vincent, E.A. *Vincent's Subdivision Map of the City of Atlanta, Dekalb County, State of Georgia: Showing All the Lots, Blocks, Sections, &c*. Savannah, GA.: Edward A. Vincent, 185?.

Watson, Traci. "Ancient Bones Reveal Girl's Tough Life in Early America." *Nature: International Weekly Journal of Science* 544 (2007): 15–16.

Weekly Constitution. "Curbstone Echoes Caught on the Wing by the Man About Town and Sent Flying Through the Constitution." April 24, 1883.

Wegener, Alfred. "Building a Case for Continental Drift." University of Illinois, https://publish.illinois.edu/alfredwegener/continental-drift.

Wells, J. & D. Appleton and Company. *Map of the Southern Part of the United States, Designed to Accompany Appletons' R.R. Guide*. New York, 1856.

Whatley, John S. "An Overview of Georgia Projectile Points and Selected Cutting Tools." *Early Georgia, The Society for Georgia Archaeology* 30, no. 1 (2002): 55–56. White, George. *Historical Collections of Georgia, Containing the Most Interesting Facts, Traditions, Biographical Sketches, Anecdotes, etc*. New York: Pudney & Russell, 1855.

Whites, Max E. *The Archaeology and History of the Native Georgia Tribes*. Gainesville: University Press of Florida, 2002.

Worth, Dr. John Fall. "The First Georgians, The Late Archaic Period (3000 B.C.–1000 B.C.)." *Fernbank Quarterly* 19, no. 4 (200): 22–30.

Wubner, Charles W. *Pioneer Citizens' History of Atlanta*. Atlanta: Byrd Printing Company, 1902.

Yates, Bobeth, "Two Arrested in Alleged Cockfighting Bust." CBS46 News, March 28, 2018.

Yukon Beringia Interpretive Centre. Government of Yukon, Department of Tourism and Culture. https://www.beringia.com.

ABOUT THE AUTHOR

 *T*he *Hidden History of Old Atlanta* is Mark Pifer's second book about local southern history. His previous book is *Native Decatur, The Earliest History of the Decatur, Georgia Area from Its Bedrock Formation to the Creek Wars.* Mark moved to Atlanta over twenty years ago and became engrossed in its local history. He currently lives in a historic home in Decatur, Georgia, with his wife, Robin, and two daughters, Ava and Sasha. Mark can often be found with a metal detector and shovel digging for artifacts in his yard or the yard of an agreeable neighbor. Look for a third book forthcoming from Pifer with the working title "The Truth about William McIntosh: A New Look at the Evidence and a Very Belated Defense for the Guilty Verdict History Placed on the Controversial Chief of the Creek Nation."

Visit us at
www.historypress.com